ECHOES FROM
ACROSS THE POND AND THE PAST...

"There is something quite Lennonesque about Mansfield's soul-searching—his tales are astonishingly clear and vivid."
—KEVIN GIORDANO, BarnesandNoble.com

"Ken Mansfield and I unknowingly shared the experience of the famous Apple rooftop session. Ken was not only working for the Beatles through their heyday, he was also their trusted friend. There is no one better equipped to tell the Beatles' story truthfully—and more important—factually, from the inside."
—ALAN PARSONS, Alan Parsons Project, Multi-Platinum producer and engineer to the Beatles/Pink Floyd

"Ken Mansfield worked in our offices in London and we crashed at his pad in Hollywood. We all hit it off immediately and he became an instant member of the Apple team. Even the Beatles took to him straight away. He is one of the few insiders left that bore witness to the highs and lows of those insane days when we ruled the world."
—JACK OLIVER, former president, Apple Records (1969–1971)

"Ken Mansfield brings us a new and closely personal perspective not only on the Beatles, but on a whole cast of characters. I lived through those Apple years with Ken and we became friends. It is a pleasure to experience so much of it all again through the accuracy of his storytelling and the clarity of his memory."
—PETER ASHER, Peter & Gordon/A&R chief, Apple Records/producer-manager (James Taylor, Linda Ronstadt, Carole King)

"Ken has a unique gift. He can take you in the room and have you sit with the folk he knows and make you one of the gang, part of the plan. And considering these folk include the Beatles, that is some doing. I respect the affection he has for our game, and what he brought to it will get you."
—ANDREW LOOG OLDHAM, manager and producer, Rolling Stones

THE
ROOF
THE BEATLES' FINAL CONCERT

BY THE MAN IN
THE WHITE COAT **KEN MANSFIELD** FORMER US MANAGER
APPLE RECORDS

Post Hill
PRESS

A POST HILL PRESS BOOK
ISBN: 978-1-64293-284-3

Published in association with the literary agency, WTA Services LLC, Franklin, TN.

Cover design by Ryan Truso

This is a work of nonfiction. Events, locales, and conversations are reconstructed from the author's memory. These stories have been retold as faithfully as possible, but all stories are those of the author and as such may be subject to discrepancies in details from actual events. However, in all cases, the author has attempted to assure that the essence of events and dialogue are as accurate as possible.

Post Hill Press
New York • Nashville
posthillpress.com

Published in the United States of America

31st July 1969.

Ken Mansfield Esq.,
Capitol Records Inc.,
1750 North Vine,
Hollywood and Vine,
Hollywood,
California 90028.
U.S.A.

Dear Ken,

Just a little note to congratulate you on your well
deserved promotion, which could not have gone to a
better man ... or a shorter one.

Thank you for looking after Apple Records.   Hope to
see you when you're here or I'm there.   Love to
Stan (Gortikov).

Yours, eventually,

FAMOUS
A /Show-Bizz Personality
(Tricks on the High Wire a Speciality).

IN DEDICATION AND FOND REMEMBRANCE

Alexis Mardas
Alistair Taylor
Billy Preston
Brian Epstein
Debbie Wellum
Derek Taylor
Doris Troy
George Harrison
George Martin
Jackie Lomax
John Lennon
John Tavener
Larry Delaney
Linda McCartney
Mal Evans
Maureen Starkey
Michael Gibbins
Neil Aspinall
Peter Ham
Ron Kass
Stanley Gortikov
Tom Evans

Not a bad apple in the bunch.
Something in the way they moved…me.

STAIRWAY TO THE ROOF

A TABLEAU OF CONTENT

PROLOGUE: Colorado From Here 1

INTRODUCTION 3

FIRST FLOOR 7
The News That Day 9
Four Bar Intro 15

SECOND FLOOR 19
Planting the Apple Seed 21
Over There 25
The Cart Before the Corps 29
Apple Blossoms 33
US to UK 39
The Apple Meetings 47

THIRD FLOOR 53
The Mayfair District 55
3 Savile Row 61

FOURTH FLOOR 67
Building Pressure 69
The Calm After the Storm 77
Sgt. Preston, Holy Heart of The Band 83

FIFTH FLOOR 89
Roofer Madness 91
Set 'Em Up, Jo Jo 97

THE ROOF 103

A Day on The Roof. 105

Moving Pictures 115

And the Band Played On... 121

Taking It to the Roof. 125

Street Scene. 131

Missing in Action 135

BRICKS AND MORTALS 143

Rough Mix 145

Rooftop Redhead 151

Get Back Girl 155

Oliver With a Twist. 163

Gentle Giant. 171

EPILOGUE: I Went into a Dream 177

Endnotes 207

Acknowledgments. 208

CONTRIBUTING FACTORS

CONTRIBUTING EDITOR

Marshall Terrill

HISTORICAL CONSULTANTS

Bruce Spizer
Mark Lewisohn
Robert Rodriguez
Stefan Granados

GENERAL EDITOR

Cara Highsmith

The Roof: The Beatles' Final Concert original text also includes some updated material and excerpts from Ken Mansfield's 2007 release *The White Book* which is currently out of print. For more Apple-related stories and visuals, visit *The White Book's* website at www.fabwhitebook.com.

PROLOGUE

COLORADO FROM HERE

THE NORTHERN IDAHO PANHANDLE, 1946

I look down at feet covered with the dust from fields and dirt roads. I look up from my beginnings here on the edge of northern Idaho's great Camas prairie. I am nine years old and this soil and the spaces within a few-mile radius are all I know. I look out at vastness and can feel timeless dimension. Our nearest neighbor is a quarter-mile away and we only see them when one of us needs help. I'm common; we're dirt poor, and we live far away from the small sawmill town down by the rivers. My companions are the fields, ravines, streams, a bothersome younger brother, and a dog named Blackie. Our toys are things we find abandoned alongside the country roads on our long walks to the local schoolhouse and usually have something to do with sticks, stones, or string. Life is simple. I am bored. I have no idea how blessed I am growing up here.

I am different, but don't know why I know that. Something is missing, deeply needed, or waiting in the distance. There's something beyond these windswept hills, but I haven't experienced enough of life to imagine what it could be.

I can't get enough music. I live for the handful of programs that feature records two or three times a week on our local radio station—

lots of weather and farm news, but the scheduling is short on songs. Neil McCracken, who lives over in the orchards, told me about this new invention called television, and so at night I stare at the small light bulb on the radio dial trying to get a glimpse of the bands and singers coming out of that little box.

I scan the Andrew Wyeth world around me, taking in vast wheat fields and canyons leading to the apparent rivers far off in the distance. The view before me opens north and west toward a vast panorama of untouched terrain. My dad likes to brag that we can see Colorado from here, even though it is in the other direction. I turn and look down the rutted dirt road that leads away from this isolated place as it makes its way out into and across the Nez Perce Indian Reservation lands that border our home. This is the vantage spot that always captures me. Mesmerized, I stare at that road to somewhere and something that I am not even trying to discover—distant people and events I can't even fathom. I am only nine years old for crying out loud...what do I know? I want a bicycle and the joy of discovering more than one treasure in a Cracker Jack box, not a philosophical adventure. I know now that I was sensing other places and experiences that weren't even in my conceptual vocabulary. It was a pulling, a calling out, a magnetic draw...a beckoning.

Kenny!...Kenny!!...KENNY!!! I am being called home for dinner and even though there is nothing for the sound to bounce off of, my name echoes across the barren landscape until it finds me in the distance. It is a hot summer day, and yet I am drawn to a deeper warmth— my mom and her meatloaf. I turn away from somewhere else...for now.

My dad gives thanks for our daily provision. We eat in silence.

After dinner, I am given an apple for dessert. I take it outside and sit on the ground beneath an open window where I can hear my mom teaching my little brother his alphabet.

A is for Apple.

INTRODUCTION

Someone asked me how I could write an entire book about one event, a happening that lasted less than an hour. But that event was more than just a matter of forty-two minutes—there was so much more.

I was there. My story is an intimate account of an exhilarating time that took place from 1968 to 1970. There are scores of books with facts and details about Apple and the Beatles, but this is about much more than that. Not only did I go up to the roof with them, I also had the privilege of becoming part of Apple's creative evolution and can uniquely share the sequence of events leading to that historic moment. It was Rock 'n' Roll providence that led me to 3 Savile Row in London's aristocratic Mayfair district and into the Beatles' realm. The day I walked up a few stairs from that fabled street and passed through the wondrous door into the Beatles' magical world and their brand-new home, my life was changed forever.

There were only a few of us who witnessed the concert on the roof up-close that day, each leaving that place with deep, life-long impressions that no biographer or researcher can understand or portray in distant words. My intent is for you to experience the depth of those feelings through my eyes. I tell this story from a unique standpoint: as a young man who came from far away to witness one of Rock 'n' Roll's most historic events from just a few feet away. I now see the incidents leading up to the moment of their last live appearance as a tapestry being created over time, until one day the last threads were tied off with the thrust of timelessness in a final performance on a cold rooftop.

You can't weave a tapestry without material. Some are woven with thread, some with colorful stories, some with elements brought from many different places, and even some that bring rich mixtures of the unusual onto an ethereal canvas of vast dimensions. Tapestries are not always created with a purpose. Sometimes scattered pieces find a place without intention, and then a magic moment integrates them into an artistic masterpiece.

That's what happened on January 30, 1969, when a beloved band and a few of their mates climbed to the top of their Apple Corps head-quarters at 3 Savile Row to share a final concert together. It seems in-conceivable that an enduring, beautiful creation of tenacious art could find a dirty, old rooftop as its palette, where destined innovation, ragged threads, and vibrant yesteryears from unrelated spaces were blended to-gether by four incredible artists into a moment that will never become unraveled in the hearts and minds of a generation.

Being there among the blessed few who witnessed that momentous event was surreal. About a dozen of us remain, and we are eternally bonded together by that moment.

I have purposely written this book from the heart, taking a less clinical approach so the reader can experience a more personal connec-tion to those times. I talk about what I felt, pass on what I observed, and repeat what I heard at the time from workmates who shared in these events. I even include some unsubstantiated hearsay to round things out. I admit I get warm and fuzzy and even winsome in my recollections. There was something so incredible about all that went on in London, and even LA, leading up to that day, and I treat it with great respect. My primary purpose is to let it be known that at the core of the apple there were real people—everyday people—who, through odd coincidence, became almost folkloric to those who were enamored by their happenstance…common, good, exciting, and unique people thrown together by benevolent fate to share the experience of a lifetime.

I present these remembrances for two distinct audiences. First, I have in mind the aficionados, the researchers, the ones who have lived and died with the events of this band—those who know all there is to know about the Beatles from listening, learning, loving, and leaving no stone unturned when it comes to all things to do with the Fab Four. I want to share the essence of what it was like to experience being there in addition to knowing about it. I have purposely avoided having trivial minutiae as the driving factor here. Instead, the feel of the phenomenon became my guiding light so the entire experience could be enjoyed and understood more deeply. Those of you who have explored this subject so thoroughly over the years deserve this expansion of insight.

And second, I extend an invitation to the wide-ranging everyday fans—those who have reveled in the joy of the most famous band in musical history and followed four guys who so beautifully invaded our ears, eyes, hearts, and lives with their unique offerings. The Beatles not only gave us songs to sing, but also left us with unforgettable melodies and lyrics that have measured the timelines of our lives for decades. It's hard not to hear "Yesterday" on the radio today without being taken back to a meaningful point in our lives...a reliving of moments with special places and memorable people that touched and changed us along the way. I sincerely invite you into the wondrous realization and understanding of how much there was to each of us during those times and how special it all was. What I discovered there is probably not what you may have expected. These were real people—maybe more like us than you ever imagined.

It is with great reverence, joy, and humility I share this experience with you.

C'mon, let's go up on the roof.

Peace and love,

Ken Mansfield
Former US Manager Apple Records

FIRST FLOOR

THE NEWS THAT DAY

It wouldn't be appropriate for me to set the stage for this story without first setting the stage for the era of the late 1960s.

Some consider this a magical time in history; although, many have thought it was the end of times. There is a lot of truth in both remembrances.

Speaking as an American, the year 1968 proved to be one of the most volatile years in the twentieth century, starting with the assassinations of Martin Luther King, Jr. and Robert Kennedy. A hail of bullets and tear gas from the National Guard marred the Democratic National Convention in Chicago, while on the other side of the country, the Black Panthers in Oakland began baring their claws and flashing their shotguns. Anarchy and confusion were everywhere. Thousands of college students openly and defiantly burned their draft cards to protest the Vietnam War. Revolution was in the air, and the youth of the day threatened to topple the government.

Even in a pretty staid place like the Capitol Records Tower, the music culture was changing before our eyes, and so were we. I can even pinpoint the exact dates when this seismic shift took place: June 16–18, 1967.

The Monterey Pop Festival was not just the first major rock festival in the world, it became the model for future festivals—Woodstock in particular.

This is easier to picture today now that we have similar festivals as models, but imagine seeing, for the first time, the thousands of flower children, hippies, peaceniks, free lovers, and freer spirits who attended this festival over a three-day period. I'm talking about a very large gathering of mostly stoned people occupying a small space of the universe at one time. In those seventy-two hours, there was nothing but music and good "vibes" filling the confines of the festival grounds. Everybody was blissed out and enjoying the tranquility of the weekend. There were no fights, no one overdosed or died, and no one was hurt. I learned later that this makeshift mini-city had no arrests during the three-day festivities. In fact, the Monterey deputy chief of police was quoted in a local paper as having said, "We've had more trouble at PTA conventions."

The irony in this situation is that Capitol Records had a reputation for being a fairly "straight" company in those days when it came to our artist roster. Much of the time I felt like a lonely voice in the wilderness when I would try to turn their attention to some of the bands playing the Sunset Strip clubs and other hole-in-the-wall rock joints in LA. For example, I wanted to sign artist Rick James and put together a racially-mixed group around him called Snow Black. Admittedly, it was very risqué for Capitol, but I wanted the company to take a chance on the vibrant street scene taking place in LA at the time. I felt that such a move would open the door to us attracting more contemporary bands to the label, and not doing so meant we held no appeal to the cutting-edge bands. Capitol was a very successful label, famous for its roster of top-tier acts, but times were changing, and we needed to climb down from our high "tower" and get down to street level because we were looking at the possibility of becoming the old folks home for once famous artists. There was a new game in town and the players had new moves and tight grooves, and it was time we started dancing as fast as we could.

In all honesty, as a company, we were vaguely aware of the Monterey Pop Festival that was coming up. It was happenstance that it was decided at the last minute that a few of us would attend the festival. One of the great things about being with Capitol was having major clout in everything we set out to do. Even though we made last-minute plans, we ended up with good accommodations at a nearby hotel and fifth-row center seats at the festival for the entire three days.

We were definitely "suits," and our business attire for the trip consisted of mainly slacks, ties, and white shirts with sport coats. Once we arrived on scene, we were stunned by what we saw. It was truly peace and love, with flower children all around the fairgrounds. They were getting high, dancing, singing, and basically just loving on each other. We stood out like nuns in a mosh pit. At the end of the first day, when we got back to the hotel, everyone who had jeans changed into them, and those of us who didn't wore our shirts untucked with collars turned up and no coats or ties. I remember washing my hair and combing it straight down in a sorry attempt at creating a "long hair" look. None of us had ever done drugs before and were not ready to even consider it at that point. But, during the course of the three days, I think we mentally (and later, emotionally), got with the program. Plus, the sweet scent that permeated the air aided in our experience, giving us some degree of contact high.

What we saw onstage is something we never could have prepared for. This was the turn of the musical century. The old way was definitely tossed out the window that weekend. I think we sat in our seats with our mouths open the entire time. It was one amazing performance after another. We had heard about some of these bands, but we weren't hip to the underlying swell that accompanied this new era of music and counter culture. Picture sitting less than fifty feet away from pumped-up performances by Janis Joplin with Big Brother and the Holding Company, Jimi Hendrix, the Who, the Byrds, the Mamas and the Papas, Canned Heat, Jefferson Airplane, the Grateful Dead, Buffalo Springfield, Otis Redding, Country Joe and the Fish, Eric Burdon and the Animals, Quicksilver Messenger Service, and more.

It was a mind-boggling array of cutting-edge, fresh, new talent. We walked back into the Tower with a whole new attitude about what was going on in the business. Capitol's only artist on the bill that weekend was Lou Rawls, which reflected where our roster was culturally at the time. Oddly enough, though, we did have the two biggest bands in the business that did not perform that weekend, but did have a lot to do with putting the festival together: the Beatles and the Beach Boys. I believe that fact was the impetus for us going there.

Paul McCartney was actually a governing board member of the festival and urged organizers to book this new breed of talent. Of course, the Beatles had been invited to perform at the show, but they had stopped touring six months before being asked, in February 1967, to help the organizers generate buzz for the new festival.

Both Paul and John took the time to draw a 7 x 12 piece of psychedelic-inspired artwork (later sold in 2015 for $175,000) that was reprinted on page sixteen of the official program, touting the festival (but also making sure to promote their new record, *Sgt. Pepper's Lonely Hearts Club Band*). It was signed by John, Paul, George, and "Howard."

Capitol's evolution into the current pop scene had been kicked off by what we experienced in Monterey, and shortly thereafter we signed the Steve Miller Band, the Quicksilver Messenger Service, the Sons of Champlin, and then added a real feather to the Capitol cap with the addition of the Band. As soon as it was announced to the public that the Band had signed with Capitol, we had immediate pre-orders in excess of 100,000 records for their debut album, a feat unheard of in those days. Revolution—cultural and otherwise—was good for the record business.

I remember being told when I first joined the record industry that it was a recession-proof business. That might draw a few laughs now, given the decimated state of the industry, but back when vinyl was king, there was more than an ounce of truth to that statement. Think about it: when times were bad, you could go see a movie or play a record to take your mind off of your problems, but you could only see a movie once and then you'd have to pay for admission again. However, you could buy an album for $3.98 and play it over and over and over again. For a few pennies more you could take a toke and take a trip while listening.

The era of the album and popular music as an art form was upon us thanks to the Beatles' *Sgt. Pepper*, *Rolling Stone* magazine, and FM radio changing the habits of millions of listeners. Not only did the music have to have a hook, but the lyrics had to possess meaning as well. The record-buying public of the late 1960s demanded more from music artists than a catchy two-minute and thirty-second single.

Suddenly, the scale of everything was—to borrow an industry phrase—off the charts, with *Sgt. Pepper* leading the way. Advances to new artists for record deals were astronomical, as were their recording budgets. I can remember when getting a gold record was a big deal for an artist; now the new standard is platinum and beyond.

The new money meant labels and concert promoters could take bigger chances, and that's why artists were now selling millions of records and playing in venues like arenas and stadiums. And this was just the beginning. It's true that, although passion drove artists into this new place, no one's eventual goal was to be a starving artist. When the really big bucks came raining down, the sky was no longer the limit and the nature of the business model for the record companies, concert promoters, and peripheral enterprises changed very quickly. Eventually creative people no longer held the power positions in the now bigger entertainment corporations and we all found ourselves working for accountants, investors, and lawyers. Don't get me started...

Perhaps the underpinning of all of this was the Vietnam War, which had a uniting effect on the youth of "Aquarius." In the aftermath of the John F. Kennedy assassination, music had become an escape for teens. The Beatles in particular had a healing effect on the nation's youth. Now, with the escalation of the war overseas and a wide generation gap between them, their parents, and political leaders they could not trust, youthful rebellion became a worldwide phenomenon. Music was the glue and the balm uniting a generation of hopeful kids who saw a bleak future ahead of them.

A revolution was taking place on the streets and within the record industry. Back in the sixties, it seemed as if everything was changing and every day was a milestone. Apple was a big part of this and no one fully realized how revolutionary the Beatles concept was until it was almost over. All this brings us to the new world the music business was living in then. Here's a snapshot of what was going on around the world the same month the Beatles commenced the *Let It Be* sessions and then headed up to The Roof:

- January 2—Australian media baron Rupert Murdoch purchased *The News of the World*, the deliberately controversial and largest-selling British Sunday newspaper.

- January 3—John Lennon's *Two Virgins* album was declared pornographic in New Jersey and, to stifle the controversy, was sold wrapped in a brown paper bag.

- January 6—Charles Manson and his Family rented a canary-yellow home in Canoga Park, California, calling it the "Yellow Submarine."

- January 11—Jethro Tull's *This Was* album debuted, advancing the progressive rock genre.

- January 12—Led Zeppelin released its eponymous studio debut album *Led Zeppelin*, which took a mere thirty-six hours of recording time.

- January 13—Bucking his manager, Colonel Tom Parker, Elvis Presley stepped into American Studios in Memphis, Tennessee, to commence recording of what became his landmark comeback sessions.

- January 18—Pete Best settled an out-of-court defamation lawsuit against the Beatles. The amount was undisclosed.

- January 20—Richard Milhous Nixon was inaugurated as the 37th president of the United States.

- January 22—Leonid Brezhnev avoided an assassination attempt by a Soviet army deserter.

- January 23—Cream, one of rock's first super groups, said farewell with their *Goodbye* album.

- January 27—Nine Jews were publicly executed in Damascus, Syria.

- January 28—USC's O.J. Simpson was the top draft pick by the NFL's Buffalo Bills.

- January 29—Jimi Hendrix and Pete Townshend waged a battle of guitars at a Brian Epstein tribute memorial show held at London's Marquee Club.

And to top it all off, this was the month the FBI began compiling a dossier on John Lennon, taking particular note of his political activities. The file included reports, memos, informant testimonies, newspaper clippings, and lyrics to his songs.

With this as the background for the shock waves created by the concert on the roof, it should be easy to understand why I am among the many who count the day on the roof as one of the most historic events in Rock 'n' Roll. With all the crazy things going on all around us, it was nice to get above it all and listen to a local band jam for forty-two minutes. All we had to do to close out all the world's clatter was shut the door and climb five flights of stairs.

FOUR BAR INTRO

I'm drawn here. Three Savile Row. It's a place of my past, a spot of wonderment, a speck on the time dial of my life that doesn't want to move. This address holds memories where the hands of time will remain frozen in place for the rest of my life. The events here were so monumental, the impressions so deep, the people so colossal in charismatic stature, that whenever I return, whether in body, mind, or spirit, I become emotionally glued to the place, the time…the moments within. I wonder why I am surprised at the cold, damp mid-day weather on this darkened street—after all, it is wintertime in London.

I stand facing the building, but not staring up at it. I am looking instead with my eyes closed, letting the smell of the street, the familiar dampness on my cheeks, and the same bustling sounds I remember hearing almost fifty years ago, come alive for me as I relive a journey that led me up a few steps to the small door stationed above the sidewalk—a beckoning threshold to another world. I know better than to gaze at the now blasphemed exterior because Jack Oliver, who, at that time, was my touch point in his position as the head of international for Apple Records, had warned me about what I would find. Serving as the original US Manager of Apple Records, I was Jack's counterpart in America. Operating from across the pond, he was the person I had the most interaction with concerning day-to-day matters. He kindly prepared me before I came here, describing what he encountered earlier when he made his annual pilgrimage back to London and his old Mayfair district job site.

If I open my eyes I will be slammed with the unwanted ophthalmic intrusion of an Abercrombie Kids store. Why not put a McDonald's in the Sistine Chapel? Same abhorrence in my mind. I do understand that lady time marches on, but why must she be such a harsh mistress? If I were in charge of all things sacred, I wouldn't have let them change anything in this special place, not even a light bulb. I admit the antics within its interior back then may have been considered child-like, but this place was never intended to be a kid's store. The only saving grace for me is that Jack said, when he hesitantly ventured forth into its tainted interior, he found that they had set aside a shrine of sorts in the lobby to commemorate its revered past. In fact, they had stacked a collection of Beatles books in a glass case, and my first book *The Beatles, The Bible, and Bodega Bay* was on top of the stack. Hallowed words resting in a hollowed place—the words intact, but the special location now gutted of its memorial impressions.

I wanted to go inside to see if I could retrace my steps, peer into the spaces where dear friends and compatriots once dwelled and dreamed, but Jack had scouted out the enemy camp and there was almost nothing left to touch upon even in silence or Rock 'n' Roll reverence. So, I keep my eyes closed and picture the daily inhabitants of old being dropped off and hurrying up those few steps, pushing their way inside, closing the portal quickly behind them to lock the outside craziness away from the madness that surely awaited them inside.

Here they come, the Apple bunch, the Beatles' buddies, the beautiful birds, workers, wannabes, and Rock 'n' Roll royalty, quickstepping in my memory march: Derek Taylor with the cocky demeanor of a rebel prince; Ron Kass with the smooth glide of a world-wise aristocrat; Peter Brown, judiciously maintaining the aloof air of a tailored Peter Ustinov; pretty Chris O'Dell, an American lass who fit in perfectly with the British beats, keeping her head down and always in a hurry; Tony Bramwell, intentionally casual and cool; Jack Oliver, smallish in stature, but big in presence and demanding respect from onlookers with only a glance; next up is Richard DiLello, the "House Hippie" with head ablaze in a massive hair storm saunters in; and, in their own time, the very quiet, contemplative Peter Asher and the bustling Kevin Harrington, each adding color to the flow with their bright red hair. And then there's "Magic Alex" Mardas, who had a jaunt to his steps that suggested he was wearing a cape and carrying a wand beneath the folds, followed by Neil Aspinall, bent forward with a firm intent that made you draw back like you would from a Scotland Yard detective or mafia hitman. And then—aaah—last but not least, I welcome the softest part of this replay, as Mal Evans arrives with the gentle gait of your friendly neighborhood dairyman, delivering his milk of kindness to the door.

Already in place, waiting inside, are receptionist, Debbie Wellum, Barbara O'Donnell, and the other secretaries, along with various assistants, people with improbable titles, and oddballs with no earthly reason for being there—all characters mixed in with a scattered variety of eccentrics and the ever-present hangers on. Movie stars, rock gods, poets, playwrights, sages, self-appointed saints, inventors, celebrity predators, pilfering pirates, belligerent bikers, and assorted befuddled masses also randomly filter in and out of this newfound musical Mecca during those heady days.

Then comes the real moving drama when a limo pulls up and George Harrison quickly hops out with guitar in hand, followed in time by John Lennon, with Yoko Ono decidedly in tow. A few beats and a dotted whole note later in the cadence of this scenario, Paul McCartney arrives carrying nothing in his hands, but sporting a big, friendly smile on his boyish face. Finally, the mood lightens even more when Ringo Starr saunters in as if he is simply showing up for work. He gives the small perpetual crowd what they have been waiting for by winking at the Apple Scruffs huddled about and throwing peace signs to the faithful and oft-bothersome tourists and fans. Engineers, gofers, and assistants are already inside the studio. Gracious George Martin may already be within the interior or will come about a little later in the manner befitting his wonderful, gentlemanly manner—a creative father figure to the lads and an inspiration to all who fall within his measured, warm gaze. Remaining studio personnel make a learned beeline for the railed steps to the left side of the main entrance that lead down to the basement and the studio below. They will emerge later in the day, leaving innovative imprints still echoing off walls drenched with their creative impressions. Some leave by the same door they came in, and some merge up into the other part of their new business empire. Instead of assuming a typical stance behind their musical instruments of choice, they make their way to individual offices and seat themselves behind desks of corporate purpose. Chaos prevails throughout the building as a typical day of matchless occurrences unfold and fill the five stories of this magic location on the time-honored Savile Row of propriety.

I am drawn in and driven back by a conflicting flood of emotions as I ponder why I had to come back here for a last look…a touch. In the youthful vibrancy of the 1960s, I knew what to do, but now…how do I get back to the roof…penetrate this off-putting child's play menagerie before me…back to a place where we all once belonged?

I am so locked into my contemplation that I probably haven't moved a muscle for an hour. I am surprised I am not mistaken for one of those curious mimes that make their money assuming motionless stances in the San Francisco Fisherman's Wharf district. I glance down at my feet and don't find any coins there, and because I am not drooling I have some assurance that just a moment has passed. Possibly I simply have been mistaken for a staid and stoic Englishman. Looking away isn't working anymore, so I glare at 3 Savile Row straight on, almost wishing my indignation would sweep over the front of the building and wash its altered exterior away, stripping away the layers until the beauty of that place is once again exposed. Everyone knows A is for Apple, not Abercrombie! I am so put off I have decided that instead of attempting to revisit the roof today I am going to retrace another part of my memory lane that led in and out of this building and go on a pub crawl from days of old. I will start with one of Paul's favorites—the Green Man in Soho—and carry on from there. It might take three or four bars, but I should be hammered by the time I reach Maxwell's Bar and Grill, a later fave in nearby Covent Garden.

SECOND FLOOR

PLANTING THE APPLE SEED

LOS ANGELES, CALIFORNIA, 1965–1966

It all began for me thanks to a key inside corporate connection coupled with an innate gift of gab. With these two things going for me I maneuvered my way into a highly sought-after job as West Coast district promotion manager at Capitol Records, Hollywood USA. I quit a well-paying, career-building position in the aerospace industry, and made a giant leap from doing computerized "Program Evaluation Research Technique" analysis for the Saturn and Surveyor satellite programs in San Diego and headed north to Tinseltown. I left that prestigious space industry job at the end of 1964, and on January 5, 1965, became a Capitol Records employee working in what I later realized was the real space industry.

In August of that same year, I found myself working with the Beatles on their second American tour. There's no explanation for why I became a continued part of the Beatles lives and future aspirations other than we just hit it off from the get-go. To be clear, I have no claim on having anything to do with their fame. I simply was in the right place at the right time in this unfolding scenario. How I came to join the ride was similar in nature to that of many other characters in this exciting drama who, through pure happenstance, also rather nonchalantly became part of the Apple Corps. The "lads" and I not only had a very good relationship as formal business associates, but in a short time we also became friends. We were intrigued with each other. For me it was their British accents, wry sense of humor, and the coolest threads I had ever seen; and, for them, it was my embodying everything they had envisioned a California dude would be like with my sun tan, house with a pool in the Hollywood Hills, cool West Coast lingo, and a champagne beige Cadillac convertible with caramel cream interior and an 8-track player in the dashboard. We only spent a few days together that first time, but one of those was a rare day off for the band, and they invited me up to their rented house in Benedict Canyon to just hang out around the pool. Everything was so fascinating about them and their lives in the UK, so when they left LA to finish the tour and head on back to London, I fanaticized about what it was like…over there.

They returned a year later in August 1966, and we picked up where we left off. Being with them at the Hollywood Bowl in '65 had been some of the most exciting moments I ever experienced in my new job, but the mood was different this time when they played gigantic Dodger Stadium on August 28. The year before seemed light-hearted, and now there was tension underlying the whole experience. The official aspects of our relationship were the same, and even though the camaraderie was still alive and well, it felt diminished in comparison to the previous year.

By 1966, the novelty of touring had finally worn thin for them. The Beatles' recording expertise had progressed to where they no longer could duplicate their sound live, and they felt their performances had deteriorated to the point where it was getting embarrassing. There was also the wear and tear of travel, time away from family, old friends, and loved ones. Plus, the sheer hysteria that accompanied them wherever they went had begun to fray their nerves. George, in particular, had mentioned his distaste for their atomic fame—how it could not sustain him—and he also became deeply concerned about his physical safety.

That same year John casually mentioned to an English reporter that the Beatles were bigger than Jesus Christ, and this candid proclamation did not go over so well in the States, particularly the Deep South. Protestors held record burnings, assembled rallies; they were banned from airplay, received death threats; and the public demanded apologies. Said apologies were offered but not fully accepted. When the

Beatles began to tackle other issues such as the Vietnam War and civil rights in press conferences, it put a target on their backs.

Everything had taken a darker turn, so, in hindsight, I can understand why our relationship felt as though it had slipped more into the "business associate" category—although still friendly, they were not as inclusive. The Beatles had already made up their minds about future tours; but, when they left the next day for San Francisco, I had no idea that their Candlestick Park show would be their last formal live performance. Because I wasn't aware of how all the heavy stuff coming down on this tour affected them, I was really looking forward to working with them again and seeing them in concert at least one more time. The sad part for me was that I had also hoped that someday Capitol would send me to London to work with them and I would get to see what it was like over there. I was now well aware that was fantasy and would never happen. Oh, well…

Oh, wait…it wasn't long after we said goodbye that seeds were being sown in their minds and a magical place called Apple had begun to grow out of the fertile soil of their imagination. The concept fully ripened on the Beatle tree in the spring of 1967 and I did get to work with them again. I did get sent to London. I did get to see them in concert…one more time.

OVER THERE

LONDON, ENGLAND, SPRING 1967

Post-World War II England's tax structure was not just brutal, it was punitive to an entity like the Beatles, who were a national treasure in more ways than one. At the time, they were one of Great Britain's greatest exports, but for every £100,000 they made, almost 90 percent of it was claimed by the government because of their tax bracket, or, as George once complained, the group had to earn £100 in order for him to buy a pack of cigarettes. He even sang about the government's way of sharing their income: "There's one for you, nineteen for me."

I imagine any US politician supporting a 90 percent tax rate today would not only be voted out of office, their corpse would be dangled from Washington, DC's highest stanchion as a warning to others.

The Fab Four's accountants informed them that if they didn't put their money into a business or corporation, they'd have to pay the "Taxman" £3 million (adjusted for 2018 values, that is roughly $22 million in US dollars).

By all outward appearances they were hugely successful—they had luxurious homes, cool sports cars, and everything they fancied was easily paid for—but they owned virtually nothing. They were overseen by attorneys, accountants, and a manager, and they employed several people. The Beatles wanted for nothing; and, if they needed something, they picked up the phone, called the accountant, and simply asked for it. "Sure," was the most likely answer, but they were naively unaware of the cost and that ultimately it came right out of their designer pockets and bank account.

So, when the Beatles made a conscious decision to stop touring and focus solely on their recording output, they had to figure out a way to financially sustain themselves as well as avoid heavy taxation. Save for investments in a high-end construction company, shares in Northern Songs (the music publishing company that held the rights to the Beatles' songs), and SubaFilms (the NEMS-run film company that controlled their film projects and promotional videos), their financial portfolio was neither diverse, sophisticated, nor impressive.

The impetus to restructure came by way of the Beatles' tax lawyers who wisely suggested they form an umbrella company in April 1967, later known as…Apple Corps, which would place each of them under an exclusive contract. Setting up this new corporation was a giant baby step in the right direction. Their new relationship, called Beatles and Co., was basically an updated version of Beatles, Ltd. They would become a legal partnership, sharing all of their income, whether from group business endeavors, concerts, or solo work; and, all the money they earned, with the exception of songwriting, would go into one pot and be taxed at a much lower corporate rate than the 90 percent taken out of their paychecks. This new partnership would bind them together for ten years on a goodwill share issue of £1 million. In a nutshell, they realized that Apple one day could "keep the taxman away."

By mid-1967, they had the necessary structure in place but didn't actually know how it would take shape. At one point in time it was suggested the Beatles form a real estate company and buy up land for a chain of record shops across England.

They discussed buying a remote island and even took a summer trip to Greece to explore the idea of building four separate homes with tunnels connecting them to a glass dome and iron tracery, which would include a creative play space and a state-of-the-art recording studio. They would live and work together, have their children homeschooled by private instructors, record music, and take vast amounts of drugs undisturbed. It sounded like a very utopian idea, but was quickly dropped when they docked at a small beach in a remote village. They found their idyllic paradise littered with large rocks and not much else. In typical Ringo fashion, he took one look, shook his head, and said, "I'm going home!"

When the Greek Island idea didn't pan out, they bandied about an idea to buy a village in England with rows of houses surrounding a village green in the middle. Theoretically, each Beatle would own a side of the square. This prelude to the Apple Corps concept suggests to me an indication of their deep desire not only to "come together," but to be together as lifelong friends.

Wisely, Paul McCartney suggested that their first commercial venture should be something they knew well, had some experience with, and had little start-up cost: a music publishing company.

After the death of their manager, Brian Epstein, in August 1967, the final form of the idea began taking shape: a multimedia company controlling all of their subsidiary interests, which included a record label, music publishing company, films, electronics, and other artistic and business endeavors they wished to pursue, such as experimental recordings. As John so succinctly put it, "We've got this thing called Apple, which is going to be records, films, and electronics." Corporate structure mavens of the future must give the Beatles props for their idea of what could possibly be one of the first true multimedia companies.

Everyone knows that if you plant an Appleseed (Johnny), when that tree begins blossoming, you do get more than just one Apple. Their money grew into a tree, and although it didn't blossom in the beginning, eventually a lot of Apple branches emanated from there.

And, yes, while it was growing, the spending was so profuse that you would think someone thought money did grow on trees.

THE CART BEFORE THE CORPS

94 BAKER STREET, LONDON, 1968

Time has shown that the concept for Apple was at least thirty years ahead of its time (to the point where, indeed, many corporations followed their lead), but the unanticipated ending of this little movie was less romantic than the opening scene. We must give them applause for intention and invention, but a barely passing grade for operation and goal realization in the beginning.

It was a great concept, but somewhere along the way the execution went awry, even though Ron Kass, Apple's chief executive, appeared to be the consummate businessman and someone who definitely knew how to think corporately. Yes, the concept was very innovative, but there were some big problems—among them was that within this multimedia concept there were multiple bosses, four to be exact. Each one had a position of legitimate and complete authority and the four horsemen were not always pulling the Apple cart in the same direction. It was not only very hard for Kass to keep things logical, it was almost impossible for the day-to-day underlings at the label to stay focused. Another really big hitch in their runaway wagon was their altruistic approach to the world of creativity.

The Beatles' plan for Apple to have an open-door policy for aspiring artists bordered on being delusional. It was kindly, caring, and generously intended but operationally…"out there." It soon became unmanageable when it came to handling and sorting through the gigantic response from worldwide aspirants of musical prowess. Attempting to separate legitimate artists from the loonies proved to be an exercise in futility when it came to the reality of sheer volume. It was indeed the befuddled masses that descended on 3 Savile Row almost around the clock.

The task of initially putting Apple together fell to the Beatles' longtime road manager Neil Aspinall and Paul McCartney. It was a monumental feat considering they didn't even have an office in the beginning. Most of Apple's business was initially conducted at NEMS Enterprises, Brian Epstein's management company. A few months later they moved into a four-story building at 94 Baker Street in London, which had been purchased as an investment property by their accountants. It was there they set up shop for Apple Music Publishing in September 1967. Terry Doran, who was in the motorcar business and a past associate of Brian Epstein, was called to come aboard to head it up, and they embarked on their first official venture: the production of *Magical Mystery Tour*. Almost all aspects of that endeavor proved to be a messy affair—a harbinger of things to come.

It wasn't long before all the crazy ideas—a chain of record stores, a magazine, a school—were eventually cast aside, except for a clothing shop they opened called the Apple Boutique, but it closed within months, dissolving and disappearing into the aromatic fog. In time, though, a logical structure for Apple was conceived and did emerge out of the "ashes."

This is not to say the Apple Boutique was a bad idea. I personally liked it, and, as with most creations by the Beatles, this one was on the cutting edge. The reality and problem with it was that it was competing as a hardcore retail venture, which meant it required more than visionaries like the Beatles to pull it off; it needed a savvy retail staff that understood the ins and outs of retail—inventory control, cash flow, limited keys to the front door and cash register, and less generous employees. Today almost every celebrity, it would seem, has his or her own line of clothing because it's a lucrative business. Not so in the Age of Aquarius. A rock band opening a clothing boutique was a novel idea, and one the Beatles were willing to explore.

In addition to limited edition clothing, the shop sold psychedelic trinkets, gadgets, records, posters, and inflatable plastic furniture. Or as Paul described it, "a beautiful place where beautiful people could buy beautiful things." Again, like Apple itself, it was an idea that was simply ahead of its time.

The Beatles employed a design company known as The Fool and paid them £100,000 to design and stock the boutique with one-of-a-kind garments, hats, and other accessories, and to decorate the building. In my opinion giving The Fool free rein of the project signed the death warrant for the enterprise the day the agreement was made. In the Beatles' defense, if The Fool had been properly managed I think that exciting store could still be there as the mothership of a large chain along the lines of the Hard Rock Cafés. I can see it now, the two enterprises side-by-side feeding off of each other.

The Fool did pull off the assignment of decorating the building admirably by enlisting several dozen art students to paint a psychedelic mural across the building's façade. However, a few months later they had to repaint the building when local merchants complained about the alluring, but out of place, three-story mural featuring an Indian goddess.

When the boutique opened in December 1967, the cool clothes and other items did "fly off the shelves and racks," which is typically a good thing in retail; but, in this case, the diminishing inventory was not accompanied by the delightful ring of the cash register as merchandise made its way out the door! So, the Apple "Blowtique" vanished less than a year later, while the more solid ideas crystalized.

At this point, Neil and Paul went on a hiring spree. That's when they wisely lured Ron Kass away from his job as Liberty Records international chief to run the Apple Records division and then appointed Peter Asher as head of A&R. Next in line was Denis O'Dell, who was brought in to run Apple Films. Rounding things out, Yanni Alexis Mardas, the Greek expatriate also known as "Magic Alex," was put in charge of Apple Electronics; and Derek Taylor, a pot-smoking, gin and champagne-loving, smooth-talking, swashbuckling figure, was placed in charge of publicity. Derek turned out to be the perfect hire, Alex not so much. Other colorful characters filled out the roster. They included office manager, Alistair Taylor; Tony Bramwell, Denis O'Dell's assistant; Jack Oliver, Terry Doran's associate; Chris O'Dell, Peter Asher's assistant; Peter Brown, once Brian Epstein's personal assistant, who basically assumed his role with Apple after Brian's sudden death; and last, Mal Evans, their former roadie turned personal assistant. This lot created one unforgettable family.

I'd had no contact with the group since August 1966, so I had no idea they were contemplating such a massive undertaking. After hearing about how these Apple seeds were sewn, and two years after my last personal communication with them, I was called upstairs to the "E" floor where the top echelon of Capitol's executives dwelled. It was the 13th floor of the building; but, I guess that sounded unlucky, so it was given its own name: the "E" floor. It was there I was informed by Capitol's president, Stanley Gorikov, that something confidential called "Apple" was brewing with the Beatles, and because of my youth and previous working relationship with them I was to be part of this new adventure at our little record company.

The seeds were planted, the die was cast, the wheels were in motion, and now my incredible education at Capitol Records—which, in its formality of procedural and business ethics, turned out to be a great teaching platform—had deftly prepared me to be launched into the greatest experience a young executive could imagine. Now I understood what earning a Bachelor of Science degree in Marketing and Foreign Trade, a stint working in the rigid requirements of the Space industry, years as an entertainer and nightclub owner, plus working my way up through the ranks at Capitol had been all about. Capitol found me in the back-alley nightclubs of LA and started me out on the streets as their West Coast promotion man. For many future top executives, time on the street has proven to be a strategic preparation component for evolving into major executive positions in the entertainment industry. It was tough out there in the trenches fighting against distant odds to break your product onto the airwaves nationwide and into the mainstream media. By the time I was promoted "upstairs" at Capitol, I was a young lion hungry for more as I circled around the curved walls of the Hollywood and Vine "tower."

Then Apple came calling—a complicated enterprise headed by a complex group of fascinating people. It was a business and pleasure company based on hearts and smarts. I had music in my heart, business in my head, and bore the bruises from the harsh realities of making it in a tough business. No wonder I felt at home jumping in with both feet and joining up with those fascinating blokes from across the pond.

APPLE BLOSSOMS

LOS ANGELES, CALIFORNIA, JUNE 1968

When the Beatles conceived Apple Records, everyone, including the other major labels, initially and incorrectly assumed that Capitol Records would distribute it. In actuality, Capitol had no more right to distribute the label than anyone else, so we had to compete with the other majors for this prize. We did have one small advantage though: the Beatles were EMI/Capitol artists, and because of contractual restrictions, distributing Apple through Capitol Records was the only way the Beatles were ever going to be on their own label in America. This fact, coupled with rather substantial, pre-established relationships and a common parent company (EMI), gave us a slight…okay, major…edge. By distributing Apple through Capitol, the Beatles were able to include 1968's "Hey Jude" as part of Apple's debut release of four single records, which also included "Sour Milk Sea" by Jackie Lomax, "Thingumybob" by The Black Dyke Mills Band, and "Those Were the Days" by Mary Hopkin (a No. 1 hit in the UK and No. 2 in the US behind the Beatles' "Hey Jude"). Technically, the Beatles were not Apple artists. Although they would be releasing their records on the Apple label in the United States, my understanding of the financial process surrounding our deal with them was that the controlling documents, contracts, accounting, and record numbers were Capitol's.

Well, as it turns out, the Apple did not fall far from our tree. You could say this was the first time an apple picked a person—that person, in effect, was Capitol's President Stanley M. Gortikov who made the Beatles feel even more at home at their already familiar US record company. The adventure had become a reality and the decision had been made…Apple was ours! This new relationship was also immensely important financially to Capitol and it cemented a continued association with the Beatles. I guess you could now say that we had all of our apples in the same basket, a vine basket—a Hollywood and Vine basket.

We also had a convenient coincidence working in our favor once the Beatles made the decision that Capitol would distribute Apple. We were getting ready to hold our annual convention in LA, scheduled for the third week of June 1968. Every salesman, field rep, district and divisional branch manager, as well as all promotion and field-merchandising managers, were going to be in one room at the same time. In addition, all the major executives and employees from the "Tower" would be in attendance.

We discussed how great it would be if one of the Beatles came to the convention and announced our new venture, so Capitol president Stanley Gortikov called Apple president Ron Kass in London to see what could be done. This was not an unusual request; in fact, it was a fairly standard occurrence that when a major distribution deal is made with a new label, one of the owners would typically appear to announce the new business relationship. The Beatles liked Gortikov and they responded favorably to his request (as businessmen). Given his charming and fun-loving personality, not to mention his business acumen, Paul was the natural choice to represent them. I loved how in future meetings or discussions he and the others always referred to industry giant Gortikov simply as "Stan" or "Stanley," but always with a tone of respect and admiration.

We arranged for Paul to be brought into town without anyone knowing he was making his second solo trip to America since their ascension to worldwide stardom. Ron Kass accompanied him on the trip, along with Apple staffer Tony Bramwell and Paul's childhood friend, Ivan Vaughn. No one except Gortikov and a few select executives, including myself, knew that we would be distributing Apple Records. As a teaser, Gortikov set the stage for Paul's appearance by announcing that we were going to have a special guest make a big announcement at the convention. I don't think anyone knew it was about Apple or that a Beatle would deliver the news in person.

Once this little item was in place, Capitol Records went all out to welcome our new partner in grand style: luxury accommodations in a private bungalow at the Beverly Hills Hotel (a.k.a. the Pink Palace), first class roundtrip air travel (TWA), plus lots of limos and LA-style love. And speaking of love...this is when I met the new lady entering Paul's life. Linda Eastman immediately replaced me as his companion at the hotel when she arrived toward the end of his stay. It's been said this is when they first fell in love. Paul's visit, although of major business importance to Capitol, actually turned out to have the feeling of a pleasure trip, with a lot of camaraderie, great food, interesting episodes, and new experiences for Paul and everyone else involved. Once it was no longer necessary to keep his presence a secret it was fun watching how he really got a kick out of entering hotels and restaurants by the front door. His visit was very relaxed and exciting—the perfect setting for developing new relationships.

The convention was in progress, and the big day, Friday, June 21, 1968, arrived. Virtually every employee was sitting in their seat waiting for the festivities to begin. It was completely dark in the auditorium. I secreted Paul from a holding suite at the Century Plaza Hotel to the hotel's convention room. As he started walking down the aisle from the back of the auditorium, we had arranged for a stagehand to bring up the room lights slowly. A long, collective gasp came out of the gathering as they began to realize that a real, live, "in person" Beatle had walked into their midst. Paul, ever the diplomat, began waving, smiling, shaking hands, and giving '60s-style high-fives to those in the aisle seats as he made his way to the stage. Simultaneously, as if by some cosmic cue, everyone started cheering, clapping, standing up, and shouting with joy. There was this incredible feeling of mutual affection between the men and women of Capitol Records and Paul McCartney. I stress mutual because it truly was a joy shared equally. The left and right brains of a phenomenon in the music business journey had come face-to-face. This was a case where them that makes the records got to meet them that breaks the records. Paul was a member of the group that had given these men and women great prestige, honor, and financial rewards in their professional and personal lives—and they were the men and women who had brought it all home for the Beatles in America.

Capitol Records USA had done a great job for the Beatles. There was no debating that America was the most important market for them to break into. Looking back now, it would seem automatic; after all, they were the Beatles. But one must remember that acceptance in the United States was not a given in those days, and many famous European acts had gone before them to face dismal failure in the land of sweet American milk and honey. In fact, because Capitol Records was an EMI company, we had right of first refusal on all foreign EMI acts for the United States, and we had passed on the Beatles four times! But, this was now many successful years later, and Paul was aware of and thankful for the job that had ultimately been done here.

When the Capitol "gang" quieted down, Paul made the announcement about Apple. The place—filled with cynical, world-weary, seen-it-all, been there, done that music reps—went absolutely berserk. I would have gone double berserk had I known that the long days he and I spent during this visit—our third time working and hanging together, with a lot of it just the two of us alone at his Beverly Hills Hotel bungalow—would have a lot to do with my upcoming and unexpected employment situation.

On the last day of Paul's visit, after finishing a full schedule of activities, we returned to the bungalow just to chill, rest up, and talk about plans for the rest of the day. I was making phone calls and reviewing paperwork while he was noodling on his guitar. When I had finished my business, he included me as a sounding board for some of the songs he was working on. After a while, he got up and went to the bathroom. The suite was laid out with a big foyer off the entry. To the left was a dining area and living room, and to the right were the bedrooms and a bathroom. Paul being out of the room, I took the liberty of answering a knock at the door and met Linda Eastman for the first time.

"Hello, may I help you?" I asked. Speaking through me, not to me, she vaguely replied, "Is Paul here?" Over my shoulder she saw Paul coming back down the hall from the bedroom/bathroom, and wham! She pushed past me like a Notre Dame football tackle to where he was, full-force embraced him, push-pulled him through the door, slammed it shut, and that was the last I saw of either of them that day. I waited around for almost an hour because I had this great idea for a line in one of the songs he was working on that I knew he was dying to hear, but finally gave up and went home. I am not quite sure what happened that night, but I do know that Linda was with us until I put them on a plane heading east—man!

The next day I drove Paul and Linda to LAX. They were flying to New York together, and then he was going on to London. After we had checked in at the airport and secured tickets and seating arrangements, Paul announced that he was hungry and opted for a hot dog (he was several years away from being a vegetarian at that point) from one of the little stands LAX used to have at the top of the escalators. Linda passed on the "decomposed cadaver tube on a roll" and opted to spend her last few minutes before takeoff capturing the sights of LAX with a new camera she had purchased on the trip. These hot dog stands were short-lived, but were strategically placed close to the gates so that people in a hurry could grab a quick bite to eat before boarding. We ordered a couple of dogs and stood at the stand and ate them. Paul McCartney normally caused bedlam wherever he went, yet no one was even aware that they were standing elbow to elbow with a Beatle while they were grabbing their fast eats.

We were headed back the gate when we were gathered up by a group of airport officials who advised us that there was a bomb threat on the plane. They explained that they had set aside a special room for our comfort so the crowds wouldn't mob Paul during the extended wait. The wait did become extended, and a couple of hours soon passed. I later found out that the bomb scare was a ruse, and they were going through Paul's luggage searching for drugs. It isn't always easy to remember when specific comments were made during private conversations, especially those that took place five decades ago, but I believe it was while we were waiting that I asked Paul how they came up with the name Apple. To this day I am not sure if I was given an honest and insightful piece of information or whether he was putting me on. Bending forward with his head lowered, and looking up at me from beneath furrowed eyebrows, his answer was swift, brief, and offered forth in a hushed tone of sincerity: "Have you ever heard anyone say anything bad about an apple?"

The airport officials found no bomb (or drugs!), and it was finally time to board. During the long wait we talked about England, and I told him how much I was looking forward to visiting London and Europe someday. At the time, I was acting in the capacity of Capitol's national promotion manager and director of the artist relations department and had no idea how involved I would become with the Apple venture in the near future. Before getting on the plane, Paul took a medallion from around his neck that he had worn during the trip and put it around mine. I had admired it earlier in the week because of its uniqueness. "You better be wearing this the next time I see you," he said. He started boarding, stopped, turned around, and added, "…in London. That's in Europe, you know!"

US TO UK

SOMEWHERE OVER THE ATLANTIC OCEAN, JULY 1968

Shortly after the Capitol convention and less than a year following the death of Brian Epstein, Apple president Ron Kass notified Stanley Gortikov that he and the "lads" wanted me to become the US manager of their chief division, Apple Records. Other divisions and artistic and business endeavors such as the ill-fated Apple boutique store accumulated quickly, but over time we came to call everything "Apple." They asked that Stanley and I join them in London for a dramatic and insightful series of Apple-related meetings.

A lot of effort had gone into planning Paul's LA trip to announce the Apple/Capitol EMI distribution deal for America, and I spent a lot of time with him as well as with Apple president, Ron Kass, during their stay. This meant I basically had more involvement with the top tier of Apple than any other Capitol Records employee at the time, with the logical exception of Stanley. Plus, I had spent quality time with all four of the Beatles during the 1965 and 1966 US tours, which gave me fairly broad exposure with the guys across the pond. But, I wasn't the only one at the company who was very involved with the project. My good friend Larry Delaney, the press and publicity chief for Capitol and someone with whom I worked side-by-side during this time, had developed what seemed to me to be an even closer relationship with Kass. Their personalities were more similar than mine, and Larry's job was very important to setting up this new endeavor. He was in regular contact with London as things began opening up. Larry was also invited to join Stanley and me on the London trip, so it was a given that he was highly regarded by both companies. I don't believe either of us ever had any sense we were in competition for the job because it wasn't until Kass's call to Gortikov that we even knew there was going to be a US Manager of Apple Records.

Acting on Kass's call, just prior to going to London for the Apple meetings, Stanley told Bob York, my immediate superior and the VP and general manager of Capitol Records, to notify me about my new position. When Bob called me into his office to give me the news that day, I was totally surprised and, in all honesty, was unable at the time to wrap my brain around what this all meant. Was I now an Apple employee in a newly created position or had I just been promoted at Capitol? Oddly enough, it confusingly turned out to be both of these things, and then some. Kass had negotiated with Gortikov that I would head up the label in America, but Capitol would be responsible for my salary and expenses. This meant there were more than two edges to this sword. I had a new job with Apple, but didn't completely shed all of my responsibilities with the mother company, which included overseeing the growing family of independent labels we distributed. No one defined my position(s) clearly; things were moving fast and there was no time for dawdling along the way to getting the job(s) done. One thing I suspected was that I would have a myriad of potential bosses: Ron Kass, Paul McCartney, George Harrison, Ringo Starr, John Lennon, Stanley Gortikov, Bob York, and, in the distance, the Capitol Industries governing board. Okay, no pressure...right? While I had a nagging suspicion that any *one* of my bosses, if dissatisfied, could unilaterally fire me (what if I did something that didn't sit right with Yoko Ono and John Lennon decided I should go?); but, what I didn't know was whether *all* of them would have to agree if I wanted a raise.

So, off we went. The three of us boarded an eastbound airplane to an adventure of great magnitude, not really knowing what to expect. Apple A&R chief Peter Asher (of Peter and Gordon fame, and an old friend of mine by this point) was scheduled to pick us up at the airport.

Gortikov's straightforward admonition on the way to LAX—that the Beatles currently accounted for approximately 50 percent of Capitol's business—kept running through my head. Fifty percent! As he subtly put it, "When it has to do with the Beatles, Ken, there is no margin for error." Later on, back at the Capitol Tower in Hollywood, Bob York once again summoned me into his office to discuss my new responsibilities. He let me know in no uncertain terms that I was to "keep it together" as far as the Beatles and the Apple staffers were concerned. But, he informed me that, in order to make my job easier, I did not have to get approvals for my travel, expenditures, or schedules. In fact, I would not even be required to explain my whereabouts or what I was doing…as long as I "kept it together" with the Fab Four.

My brain was on the verge of shorting out because I couldn't imagine what my new position would evolve into, and had no hope of getting any clarity until we all sat down together in London. Our first day together was when I learned that I would indeed have four Beatles as equal bosses, and that is also when it really sunk in that my job description would probably never be clearly defined. Because I still would be working mainly out of my Los Angeles Capitol Tower office, I wondered what my working relationship would be like with my teammates at Capitol. Procedures were always very rigidly in place at this large corporation and my new marching orders were going to be unique to the organization.

My mind was racing as the plane was racing to a new destination for me. We were on a red-eye to London from LA, but I couldn't sleep. I remember peering out the little oval window into the clouds searching for the coastline. Still in a state of disbelief at the recent dramatic upturn in my career, I tried to discern the transitional point in my life that brought me out of a small town in northern Idaho into this moment and this airplane as it prepared for the approach to Heathrow Airport.

When the runway finally came into sight, the view from the oval window looked cold, rainy, and bleak. It wasn't until the wheels touched the ground that it all suddenly hit me—here I was…London, England, Europe…the Beatles! This was really heady stuff, and this country boy was scared stiff.

Thank God it was Peter Asher who met us at Heathrow. After our mini-reunion, which included my inquiry into the well-being and whereabouts of my friend and his ex-partner, Gordon Waller, I began to feel relaxed, like I was among friends. Peter adeptly ushered Stanley, Larry, and me curbside at Heathrow where he presented us with our uniformed chauffeur, who snapped a curt salute as he held forth stiffly in front of our personal white Rolls Royce limousine. Apple had graciously provided this classy perk for us, available on a twenty-four-hour basis for the entire visit. We were then driven (without our baggage because, naturally, someone was tasked with seeing that it was properly delivered) to our waiting suites at the Royal Lancaster Hotel in the Westminster Borough with rooms overlooking Hyde Park. Of course, we were preregistered, pre-checked in—pre-Fabbed in every way. Getting to experience this together was special to Peter and me because we had become good friends during the "Peter and Gordon" visits to California (they were signed to Capitol in the United States), where my responsibility as head of promotion and artist relations was to spend the entire time with them during their visits and tours. I would meet them at the airport in Los Angeles and cart them off to their hotel. Now he had met me at the airport and had just delivered me to my hotel.

There was a continuous irony to our relationship in how our paths crossed repeatedly. After the Peter-and-Gordon era and our Capitol Records stint, we ended up at Apple, and then years later we became vice presidents at MGM together, which was followed by us both leaving the loony lion to eventually become independent record producers. To give this sequence of events a perpetual feel, as record producers we both scored chart-topping singles at the same time with similar artists (Linda Ronstadt and Jessi Colter). Coincidentally, but not surprisingly, we then found ourselves mixing our competitive hit albums side by side in the same town (Hollywood) at the same studio (The Sound Factory) for the same record label (Capitol). That was followed by the unusual circumstance of becoming head-on competitors for the first time as both single records (Jessi's "I'm Not Lisa" and Linda's "You're No Good") ended up in Billboard's Top 5 fighting for the No. 1 slot on the Hot 100 pop chart.

The chauffeur became a regular member of our entourage during our visit; and, as protocol would dictate, he never spoke to us first—he would only respond when a conversation was initiated on our part. His answers would be to the point and always courteous. If he did need to make an unsolicited comment (like if my hair was on fire or something), he would always ask permission to speak before actually doing so. We would sometimes keep him going for twenty-four hours in a row, and he was always crisp, polite, alert, and available to serve us at all times—no complaints, just proper demeanor and courtesy.

So, there I was, London, England, August 1968, summertime, ensconced in a beautiful hotel when…knock, knock. I open the door. "Hello, my name is Peter Brown, and I am the chief of protocol for the Beatles. I have come to give you your *shejule* [schedule]." He then continued on officiously, outlining the said *shejule* without any response from me or even a little transitory chitchat. His approach was proper, clear of purpose, and very, very English. There was no question that we would be spending quite a lot of time communicating with each other over the months or years ahead, but right now he had an agenda, and we were going to discuss my…*shejule*.

When Peter Brown came to my door, I was still looking out the window at my beautiful view of the park, listening to the stereo system and admiring a large selection of current English rock albums piled up in my room by the Beatles' personal staff.

"At 13.00 hours the Rolls Royce will once again pick you, Mr. Gortikov, and Mr. Delaney up and take you to the Ritz Hotel for lunch, where you will be joined by the four Beatles, Neil Aspinall, Mal Evans, Ron Kass, and myself.

"At 14.30 hours you will be taken to the new Apple offices at 3 Savile, where you will be welcomed by Alex Mardas and Derek Taylor, who will give you a tour of our new offices and allow you the opportunity to meet some of the staff. After that you will be given the opportunity to hear songs the lads have recorded for their new album. Tea and a buffet catered by Fortnum and Mason will available during this time.

"At 17.00 hours you will be returned to your suite and allowed time to rest and freshen up for the evening activities.

"At 20.00 hours the Rolls Royce will drive the three of you to the Queens Theatre, where you will be joined by John and Yoko, Neil Aspinall and Susie, Ron Kass, and Peter Brown. You will be seeing a new play, 'Halfway up the Tree' starring Robert Morley, written by Peter Ustinov, and directed by John Gielgud." (Now here is where my memory and another reported version of this evening collide. My recollection is that it was Ringo Starr and Maureen who actually joined the entourage that evening, and I was very surprised when I read somewhere that they were not there, but that it was John and Yoko who had attended.

I was so disturbed by this contradiction of facts and what I felt was my clear recollection, that I got in touch with Stan Gortikov shortly before he passed away to find out how he remembered the event. He said he couldn't say for sure that Ringo and Maureen were there but said he would have definitely remembered if John and Yoko were, and he did not recall them joining us at the theatre.)

"Tomorrow we will begin at 13.00 hours by enjoying brunch with all four of the lads (and Yoko) in the private restaurant at your hotel that has been reserved for just our group to get better acquainted. Then we will go directly into meetings for the rest of the day. Upon conclusion of the meetings you are free to return to your suites and spend some time of your own choosing. Later on, Paul has offered to take anyone who would like to join him, out on the town for night clubbing." Peter Brown clearly laid out our whole itinerary for the entire visit with the perfect blend of subtly tourist things and hip insider jaunts that would help meld us into the organization. There was also the obvious proper mixture of time being with all four Beatles together and one-on-one, spent in various activities.

I liked Peter Brown a lot upon this first meeting. He reminded me of a regal rock and proper roll version of Peter Ustinov. I was to learn as time went on that his proper British demeanor had, over time, replaced a common upbringing akin to some of the other members of the Apple Corps. After returning from my visits there, the guys back at the home office in California often commented (sarcastically but fondly) on how classy I had become in manner and speech, maybe emulating Peter. You can't spend any length of time working in London, especially when surrounded by a gang made up of a lot of Liverpudlians (scousers) without returning home with a bit of a British accent and inapt swagger. Unfortunately, the Capitol gang would howl in kindhearted disgust when I would try to interject the word "shejule" into our planning meetings back in LA.

The point is Lennon, McCartney, Harrison, and Starr had skillfully orchestrated, and helped co-arrange the perfect song and dance to bring our two worlds together into a relaxed and meaningful business-working association. There was more than one reason for my being brought to London in addition to the planning meetings and other important business matters. They were very smart as businessmen; they already had schmoozing down to a science. I knew the American market and was well-versed in making the moves needed to get the Apple rolling up a very steep and competitive hill. The Beatles were already successful and needed no help. Job one was establishing Apple as a viable new record label and breaking new, unfamiliar acts to the public. They let me know they had great confidence in me, and that gave me a sense of importance in accomplishing their mission. I was warmly invited into one level of their inner circles and had been made to feel I was part of the gang. By the time I left for home, they had me so pumped up I was ready to walk through walls for our new company.

The Apple had polished the teacher!

THE APPLE MEETINGS

ROYAL LANCASTER HOTEL, HYDE PARK, LONDON W2

You would think that trying to schedule and hold formal meetings with the members of the most commercially successful four-piece Rock 'n' Roll band in the world would be like trying to organize fire ants into straight columns, but it was quite the opposite with the Beatles. They had achieved about every marker of success possible in popular music, and they took the Apple endeavor very seriously. After all, it was their money and future at stake.

Over the years, I've wished some of my other business associates could have been as punctual and attentive (also as enthusiastic) to the matters at hand as they were. Their fame and fortune allowed them to become businessmen and they were not playing around. They really enjoyed this new endeavor in the beginning and were truly into it on all levels. As crazy as the whole thing was, I defy any other group of this stature to be as focused and coordinated in effort and spirit as this one was at the outset.

Apple was fun. Apple had heart and a philosophy of good intent. It had good people and good music. I wish it could have gone on forever with the same heart, same intent, and especially the same people.

They had reserved an additional suite for the week at our hotel (the Royal Lancaster), and that is where we met. Looking back, I am still surprised how small the suite was in light of the importance of the meeting, the level of those in attendance, and the combined financial means available to select a more conducive setting. On the other hand, the subtle discomfort made it very personal and may have been intentional to foster the feeling of closeness that appeared to be part of Apple's agenda for this new business union.

The days were long and we all worked hard. It was an official Apple planning meeting with the four owners of the company (John, Paul, George, and Ringo,) Neil Aspinall, Mal Evans, Peter Asher, Ron Kass, Yoko Ono, and us three Capitol executives—Stanley Gortikov, Larry Delaney, and me. (On a somber note, of the twelve people in those early meetings, only five of us remain at this writing, and similar statistics pertain to those who were on the roof months later.)

We would break for lunch in the showroom on the top floor—a classic English supper club that featured dining and dancing to a four-piece band, which was only open in the evenings. We enjoyed our noon meal there without the intrusion of fans during these much-needed breaks.

Stan, Larry, myself, and the other Apple staffers got a surprise musical treat one day during our secluded mid-day break. We were seated at a table in front of the empty bandstand, and, as we were finishing lunch, Paul got up from the table, stepped up on the small bandstand, sat down behind the piano, and began laying down a cool groove. Before long, all four Beatles were on stage jamming, and they played a twenty-minute impromptu set for us—their delighted guests. I have no recollection of what songs they played that day, but being able to watch and listen to our new employers having a good time during their lunch break was completely surreal, especially when you consider it was our very own, exclusive Beatles concert.

During the nonmusical portion of these meetings, we decided that when I returned to the US, I would set up a six-man promotion team to operate regionally. This team would be drawn from the elite of Capitol's fifty-man field team that I had put together over the years as national promotion manager for the label. I knew every man well because I had hired most of them personally. Gortikov approved this team as a Capitol expenditure, and felt that the other half-dozen small independent labels that I was still responsible for could use this promotional swat team's efforts as well. We decided on the first four releases and mapped out the original release campaign. We then decided it would culminate in the "Golden Apple" Award ceremony that was subsequently held in LA at the then-happening Sunset Strip Playboy Club. The Playboy Club—my how the times have changed.

The meetings were informal yet serious at the same time. There were a lot of important matters to cover and resolve at this gathering; yet, even with all that pressure, there was also a sense of intense calm. Something kept happening in the conversation that caught my attention by the very fact of its repetition. This particular phrase was simply two words that were used by each one of the Beatles, not only during this meeting, but also at other times when I would be with them one-on-one. That phrase was simply: "the Beatles."

As we discussed promotions, concepts, and upcoming releases on the Beatles and other Apple artists, each of the four in turn would refer to the Beatles as if we were

The basic concept of the competition between Capitol's field promotion staff for the Golden Apple Award was based on a formula for airplay and sales on a territorial basis. The promotion man who got the most airplay on designated key stations in his district and created the most sales on the first four Apple releases would be flown first class to LA. There he would be rewarded with a banquet in his honor and presented a large, beautiful, gold apple as a trophy. When we were planning this event at the Apple meetings in London, the Beatles agreed that the icing on the cake for this award would be that one of them would fly in from London to present the Golden Apple in person. Some of the employees were a little suspicious when the LA promotion man won the contest. They also felt it was a little more than coincidental that George just happened to be in town during that time. It did appear a little convenient, but it helped the Beatles keep their promise.

discussing a band that was from another planet. I asked Paul why they kept referring to the band in the third person. He explained to me that the whole "Beatles" phenomenon had exploded into such a tremendous abstract anomaly that it had gone beyond them to the point that it became something bigger than they could comprehend. As we sat in that room there was a "them," that is to say, a John, a Paul, a George, and a Ringo; then there was this other enigmatic thing known to the world as "the Beatles." Things like this really distilled the essence of the whole atmosphere surrounding their celebrity and the way they viewed their fame. I was so amazed at how normal and easy it was to be with, and work for, these four guys. "The Beatles" was a giant superstar group, while they were simply themselves.

Probably the most memorable part of the meetings was Paul's personal dilemma over the first Beatles release to be included in the "First Four." Although the "A" and "B" songs had been selected ("Hey Jude" and "Revolution"), Paul had serious misgivings about the acceptability of the length of "Hey Jude," which clocked in at over seven minutes. The reason for his concern was the fact that in America Top 40 radio stations were in a heated battle for ratings and the surest way to get listeners was to play the most hits every hour. The stations became the tail that was wagging the record companies' and artists' dogged efforts to get airplay. If we presented a record over two and half minutes in length, there was very little chance for airplay, because it ate up too much of their time and thwarted their claim to being the station that played the most hits every hour. So, in a short amount of time we all—songwriters, arrangers, producers, artists, editors, mixing and mastering engineers, and record labels—were forced to comply with this requirement, and it changed the way we thought about the music. This whole scenario had a major effect on the promotion and marketing teams' efforts to establish new artists.

After our Royal Lancaster Hotel meetings, we would adjourn to the new Apple building on 3 Savile Row, where a professional tape deck and giant sound system had been set up in one of the larger rooms. The building had recently been carpeted in dark green and the entire interior painted white. There was no other furniture or accouterments except for a table set with refreshments and snacks at the opposite end of the room. We would sit on the floor for extended periods playing those two songs over and over trying to decide if we wanted to buck the system by releasing "Hey Jude" as the "A" side. We were going to play by the rule that all new releases had the "A" and "B" side designated for Top 40 airplay purposes.

The perfunctory reason for clearly designating the "A" and "B" sides was so that when a record company released an artist's new record, the promotion men would all work on the same song (the "A" side) for airplay in order to create a hit song. For example, if 100 percent of the important radio stations played one side of a record, it meant you had a hit. If 50 percent of the stations played one side and 50 percent played the other side, it meant you had a mediocre chance at success. The irony of this dilemma was that every station played every song the Beatles released. They were going to play both sides anyway, but Paul wanted to do it by the numbers. It was amazing to sit on the floor in front of the speakers and witness Paul's artistic insecurity. Somehow, fear of rejection didn't seem an appropriate emotion in that room. (Looking back, one thing I find great joy in is the fact that I don't remember any of the Beatles ever suggesting that one alternative to this problem would be to shorten "Hey Jude.") At that point in their careers they could have belched "Tie a Yellow Ribbon Around the Old Oak Tree" with an accordion band and had a hit.

It seemed the playbacks would go on forever until I came up with a suggestion that put Paul at ease. I volunteered to reroute myself on the way back to LA via a few key airplay markets if he would trust me with one advance copy of the record. I would hopscotch my way across America after leaving London, going first to Philadelphia where I would play it for Jim Hilliard at WFIL. Next I'd continue to Jim Dunlap at WQAM in Miami, and then head out to St. Louis and a couple other major cities before ending up in LA at KRLA with music director Dick Moreland. These men and a few others at American Top 40 stations at that time were known and respected for their ability to "pick the hits." The plan was for me to call Paul when I got back to LA and let him know the results. He liked the idea, and I really liked the idea because not only was it a very exciting first assignment, but also a great PR move for me with some major radio stations. Needless to say, the music directors fell out of their chairs when they heard "Hey Jude." Such a hesitant start to possibly their greatest record! When I got back to LA I called Paul and it was a go.

At the conclusion of the meetings at the Royal Lancaster Hotel, the Apple contracts were signed by Gortikov and the four Beatles right there on a small table in the suite. Then the Beatles presented us with hand-lathed 45 rpm copies of the first four records. They had packaged them in individual black plastic boxes embossed with our names— Stanley Gortikov, Larry Delaney, and Ken Mansfield—a green Apple,

"Our First Four," and 3 Savile Row on the front. One thing that made the package even more special was that the labels on the records were handwritten by the Beatles themselves. For Capitol's part, Gortikov had arranged to present them with a special crystal Apple. It didn't make it to the meetings, so he symbolically presented them with a real apple instead and a crystal rain check in return. This real apple had been placed in the center of the table with the documents. After the contracts were signed, Paul picked up the apple, walked away from the others, and ate it.

The first four records to be released on Apple were the Beatles' "Hey Jude" backed with "Revolution;" Mary Hopkin's "Those Were the Days" backed with "Turn, Turn, Turn;" Jackie Lomax's "Sour Milk Sea" backed with "The Eagle Laughs at You;" and the Black Dyke Mills Band's "Thingumybob" backed with "Yellow Submarine." The advertising agency Wolfe and Ollins designed the "Our First Four" plastic 10 x 12 black matte box. This special package also contained photos and bios along with the records. Many years later, during some very lean times in Nashville, I had to decide between looking at that package and eating. This unique treasured gift from the Beatles represented a time in my life when I felt very alive and vital. In Tennessee, in order to be vital, I had to sell it for "vittles" to stay alive, so I sold it for a few hundred dollars. Years later Stanley Gortikov's son sold his copy on the Antiques Roadshow TV program for $60,000.

Years later, after the breakup, I was rummaging through some old boxes in my closet and out fell a picture of Paul standing apart from the others, back turned to them, staring out the window and finishing off the apple. Interesting, and perhaps a little foreshadowing of what was to come...

If I had been able to wait, that could have put more than vittles on my table!

THIRD FLOOR

THE MAYFAIR DISTRICT

In order to get a deeper sense of the Beatles last concert on the roof, I believe it is valuable to get a feeling about the venue for the concert. The concert did take place at 3 Savile Row, but the broader geographical setting where this event occurred was the upscale Mayfair district in central London's business district. Mayfair was definitely not the typical location for an outdoor rock concert at that time, especially one being performed by the most famous rock band of all time, and a freebie concert for the public at that. If this concert took place in a warehouse in a rundown industrial area in the San Fernando Valley it would have had an entirely different effect on its surroundings and the people who were touched by it. A good analogy would be a diamond for an engagement ring that, when carefully mounted in the right setting, becomes more attractive, has more effect, or can even appear bigger than it really is. Put a warthog in a posh boutique on Madison Avenue and its appearance will have a more dramatic effect than it would in its natural setting in sub-Saharan Africa. You have to admit the contrast of the setting for this event did put an edge and a little sparkle dust on the whole rooftop affair.

There is a bit of incongruity concerning the venue and the occasion, so that's why I think it not only relative but important to take a look at Mayfair. My starting point will be based on a question asked by Christopher Middleton in a recent "London Telegraph" article: "How did a boggy meadow turn into one of the most exclusive and expensive postcodes in Britain?" In answer to that simple query I am briefly and mainly drawing on information from author/modern-day Mayfair real estate mogul Peter Wetherell's book *The Story of Mayfair*. Peter's analytical treatise gave me an idea and an understanding of this special place. Like the building at 3 Savile Row, I wish I would have known more about Mayfair when I ventured forth into its realm back then. As you read on I think you will understand why.

Today, Mayfair is the home of some of Britain's most expensive property, but circa 1675, it was a nondescript patch of open ground made muddy and boggy by the River Tyburn. Suddenly though, in 1686, the area acquired not just a name, but also a purpose. King James II granted permission for a fair to be held there during the first two weeks of May. (Hmm. I wonder what a good name for a fair held in May could be?) People had recently escaped the grip of the Great Plague and took the opportunity to come to this meadow to let their hair down. Before long, the "May Fair" became a byword first for music, dancing, and merriment, and then for what the authorities termed "disorderly practices." (Maybe the Apple enterprise being located there and the concert on the roof are not so incongruous after all.)

But in passage of time Mary Davies, the daughter of a wealthy banker, inherited 100 acres of these "swampy meads," which had now found itself situated just south of Oxford Street and east of Park Lane. Mary married into the Grosvenors, a powerful, Cheshire-based landowning family, and the seeds of modern-day "Mayfair" were sown. Next in our condensed timeline, upscale Grosvenor Square was constructed while all around it the aristocrats were developing nearby Brook Street and Hanover Square. As Wetherell so succinctly put it, "All of a sudden, those meads were becoming not swampy, but swanky." Grosvenor Square was the crown jewel of the district and became a magnet for dukes, earls, viscounts, and marquises. According to Wetherell, "Of the initial 277 houses, 117 had titled owners."

But centuries passed, including two world wars, epidemics, and up and down turns of every kind, until eventually the area's mansions were turned into office buildings and put to other commercial use. By 1939, three-quarters of Mayfair's houses were being used for business purposes and this conversion of property continued during World War II. But now, according to Peter and counter to my impression, they are once again being returned to residential use.

I know I am imposing quite a bit of import on the "setting" for the roof concert, but this offers some understanding for why I feel this awareness is important to that day. While it does seem to reek of a lot of semi-interesting "era" facts, I am actually just skimming the surface. January 30, 1969 was really, in its own way, the ending of an era. When I think of those four guys playing in the cold up there above the somewhat stodgy street for the last time—an oddly exciting time filled with turmoil over realized dreams and emotions they never thought they would experience—I can't help but ponder where they came from and their ordinary personal histories. Before me lies the back story of that street, that district, and their two histories colliding into sharing a "top of the pile" uniqueness, and I become mesmerized. Let me continue the thought in the form of a discussion. This is something I never discussed in detail with the four of them then (and I obviously cannot do so now), so I will go over it with you. My thoughts come about in reaction to something I covered in past books.

During the early Apple meetings, I was struck by the fact, partly from conversations with them as well as my own surmising, that they wanted to expand their public persona by becoming upscale, legitimate business entrepreneurs and proper corporate gentlemen. Those descriptive words of categorization are mostly mine in painting the picture of them I saw unfolding before me, but it was also given depth by their own words—words I read an expanded meaning into. They explained that one of the driving energies behind creating Apple was the fact that in their line of business they had no more substantial goals. They couldn't become more number one—they were at the top of the heap, living as high on the mountain as you could get. Wealth, recognition, musical innovation accomplishments, and personal satisfaction of a "job well done" in their craft were all crossed off their "life's desires" bucket list. They also may have had just a little crunch in their craw over people and instances where they had been misled, mishandled, or mistreated in business matters in the past. I mean (sarcastically of course) what do Rock 'n' Rollers know about such intellectual matters as contracts, marketing, financial matters etc. when they are young and naive? As we all know now, these guys weren't stupid, so what took place in creating Apple involved their personal creativity, a passion within that was driving them to continued ground-breaking activities, and a heightened sense of value. I have a feeling there could have been a smattering of getting even with some of the naysayers to their talent along the way.

Bear with me because I am finally getting somewhere here, and it all leads to the roof. If the Beatles were going to take a step up, they weren't going to set up shop in a tawdry area. Buying and being on Savile Row in the Mayfair district showed they had good taste and were serious about their new adventure. Let me also interject a quick insignificant observation at this point. Over the years I have worked with a lot of rock bands, and it was common in many cases (though not all instances of course) that the more successful they became the sloppier their appearance and clothing became. In contrast to that, Paul and Ringo always blew me away with how well they dressed. Look back over the years and you'll notice that Paul favored cool slacks and sports coats over jeans, T-shirts, and the dark leathers of the Cavern days. Ringo was always dressed in the latest threads of cutting-edge fashion attire, and in the early years John and George would often lean to the perfect mix of contemporary conservative and hip garb. Like so many of us, they grew up common but were common no more. Proof of their creative bent, intellectual prowess, and innate moxie, and I believe the crowning achievement in this new corporate world they were entering, is what they did in structuring Apple Corps. As stated earlier, they did something copied by many major companies today, making them true innovators in the way they put together their business plan. They moved their entire asset-creating abilities and enterprises under one corporate umbrella in order to take charge of their lives. I think a perfect example of how this works would be something like McDonald's owning their own potato farms and controlling their french fries.

Anyway, I backtracked into this discussion/musing by something that happened to me when I first got out of a White Rolls Royce limo at the Apple offices front door. Here is what I'm talking about...

When reading about the geography and location of this event I was suddenly made aware of a street level (pun intended) feeling I would have when I went to 3 Savile Row from either the airport or a nearby Hyde Park hotel where I was staying. I didn't know then how upscale, ritzy, and historical the Mayfair district was, and had been for centuries. All I knew was that when I was dropped off at the front door and looked up at that building and the few steps leading up to its door I felt like a kid who was standing in a place where I didn't belong. Without realizing it then, my own Idaho potato head upbringing sensed that I was still common and out of place there on the "Row."

Everything was so proper up and down that street and the immediate surroundings, but when I walked through the door into the offices I found a vibrant, chaotic place nestled amongst the glamour of British propriety, and when I closed the door behind me I felt at home. The thing I really liked, but didn't understand at the time, was that, maybe because of the street, going in and out of that building did make me feel like I was somebody.

So, Mayfair is more than a district; Savile Row is more than a street; and 3 Savile Row is more than just a building. It is a setting…the setting where history of a different kind was made. Because of where and what it was, it took hold of me in a way that can't be completely explained. Maybe this is what I was trying to see in the distance when, as a nine-year-old kid, I stood mesmerized, staring at…a road to somewhere and something that I wasn't even trying to discover—distant people and events I couldn't even imagine.

3 SAVILE ROW

A HOUSE IS NOT A HOME IF NO ONE'S LIVING THERE

Three Savile Row was built as a home, and that's what it was all about for most of its early life. Because so many of its inhabitants were so fascinating, they have imbued the place with a fantastic history. But places, like people, change, and, like people, their purpose and character evolves beyond original intention. Originally, 3 Savile Row was a place called home: a place of gathering, a place where friends would sit in easy chairs by one of many fireplaces, a place where families and memories grew up together.

Then there came a new time where its rooms had different purpose and people of a different resolve filled the chairs. There was business to be done and those chairs were gathered around desks and conference tables while new bonds were created around new goals and growth. This was a time where strangers gathered to form a different kind of family that also strived to live and grow together. Exciting innovations were the order of the day for a business family.

The difference between these two eras is what happened at the end of the day. The early inhabitants closed the front door at eventide and nestled within its warm interior for the night as a family while the succeeding occupants closed that same door and left behind an empty place, no longer a family. The chairs remained, but no one was sitting there.

When the Beatles were given the keys to the front door all these things and more returned to this place—history, innovation, business, gathering, excitement, and a sense of family were ushered in with them. Also, history was once again created there and you could feel its passion radiating from the walls.

And that front door...once the Apple Corps made that place their home, though it may have been locked at times, in a sense it was never closed. I now invite you to come on in and meet that remarkable building. Once you have a feeling for its structure, history, and growth, it will become like a magic dollhouse where you can, with reverence and joy, place its people and events back where they once belonged.

So, before we "get back" to the music and go up on the roof, let's "go back" a few centuries for a quick history lesson on our Apple dwelling. The Beatles weren't the first famous occupants...not by a rim shot. The five-story traditional Georgian townhouse was built in 1735 and fronted by iron railings with a small flight of stone steps leading up to its entrance.

I offer the following background of this building from my understanding of events, and if my portrayal is not 100 percent accurate and more poetic than factual, so be it. It works for me because it more clearly matches the creativity and romanticism that surrounded the impressions and experiences I enjoyed during my time in its interior. This book's intent is personal and, after poring over varying accounts of the building's history, I like the version I have come up with best.

The first owner of renown was John Forbes, Admiral of the Fleet in the British Navy. Despite a war injury that left him unable to walk, Forbes ran the Navy from his house at 3 Savile Row, which he first occupied sometime around 1760. Twenty-four years later Katherine, one of his twin daughters, exchanged nuptials with 3rd Lieutenant William Wellesley-Pole inside the home in front of esteemed guests, including the Duke of Wellington. He died in this home in 1796 at the age of eighty-one.

After Forbes's death, Katherine and William inherited the townhome but decided to live elsewhere and rented out the place. One of their tenants was Robert Ross, a well-known British general best remembered for crossing the Atlantic with an expeditionary force, kicking our (US) butts at the Battle of Bladensburg and torching the White House. I guess you could say famous Brits who took up residence in this notorious abode stormed America twice: Ross, the general who was famous for "burning down a house" and later, the Beatles, the band famous for "bringing down the house" (in America and the rest of the world). General Ross lived at Savile Row until 1805. Nearly a decade later, an American sniper's bullet took his life in a battle near Baltimore. (Payback for burning down the Executive Mansion?)

A brief but important occupant at 3 Savile Row was the aforementioned Field Marshal Arthur Wellesley, 1st Duke of Wellington. The popular war hero stayed at the swanky London digs before heading off to France. And it was a good thing he went: he was the man who went down in the history books as the man who defeated Napoleon at the Battle of Waterloo in 1815. Afterward, he found much nicer digs at Walmer Castle in Kent, England, constructed by Henry VIII in the sixteenth century. He lived there until his death in 1852. He was eighty-three.

The history of the house that made the most noise—until the Beatles took it over—was its occupancy by the voluptuous and sexy Lady Hamilton. Her real name was Amy Lyon, but she went by Emma Hart. She was a former actress and model who provided ample curious copy for local history books. A distinction that separates our two most interesting occupants, the Lady and the Lads, is the clearly verifiable factual history of the Beatles' tenure there, contrasted with the oft-contested extent and nature of "Lady Hamilton's" existence at that location.

Amy Lyon, a.k.a. Emma Hart, a.k.a. Lady Hamilton, was the muse of painter George Romney and the mistress of Admiral Lord Nelson, Britain's greatest Naval hero. It was widely rumored that he conveniently ensconced her there for a period of time at 3 Savile Row near his Bond Street home. She was described as charming, beautiful, vivacious, exceedingly good-humored and amiable. She and Lord Nelson carried on an illicit affair, despite being married to others, for a six-year period and produced a child out of wedlock.

Their liaison (which later evolved into marriage) was one of the era's great scandals. Newspapers and rag sheets dogged their every move, but also looked at Lady Hamilton as a trendsetter, reporting on the clothes she wore, the parties she threw, and the life she led—a rakish precursor to Lady Diana Spencer if you will.

War called Lord Nelson back to duty and permanently separated them. A marksman on the quarterdeck of the British flagship HMS *Victory* shot him on October 21, 1805, during the Battle of Trafalgar. His last words concerned Lady Hamilton and their daughter.

Lord Nelson's £800/month pension ensured a modest lifestyle for Lady Hamilton after his death, but she didn't know how to curb her spending habits after such a lavish lifestyle and fell deep into debt—so deep, in fact, that she was placed in a debtor's prison for a year. She moved to France to escape her debtors and lived in abject poverty until her death from dysentery in 1815. She was forty-nine.

Almost a century later the house was converted into The Albany Club, a swanky gentleman's nightclub that featured snooker tournaments and produced some of the biggest bandleaders of the era, including Jack Hylton, Britain's equivalent of Benny Goodman. The 1930s-era nightclub lived well past its expiration date when Hylton bought it November 1955. He did his best to keep the club alive but had to shutter its doors a year later. The bandleader, producer, and entertainment impresario moved all of his business operations there, which housed his theatrical management firm, and it became known as the "Hylton House." In true showbiz fashion, he turned the lower floor into a mock nightclub to prepare for his next venture: television. He capitalized on the burgeoning popularity of television and the fledgling commercial market and had a good run.

But the fun and games came to an end in January 1965 when Hylton died of a heart attack at age seventy-two. Near the end of his life, his generosity, largesse, and spending habits dwindled away a good portion of his fortune. He told his son Jack, "I won't leave you much, but we'll have a good laugh spending it while I'm here!"

I know I have gone into great detail about this building, which may seem unnecessary, but I had zero idea about its history when I got there. And yet, like the district it was in and the street outside, the reason I give it so much space is that, even in my unknowing, I could feel its history when I came to this place. It hit me when I walked through the door. I attributed this overwhelming feeling, in part, to the intense fame of its current occupants; but, now I know that this was a place of monumental destiny, and it painted whoever dwelt there with a shade of timeless destiny. There would have been no roof if there weren't something powerful to hold it up. Abstract thought, yes, but maybe that's what I sensed.

I came there alone but left with this place and its antiquity "on me." I also know that the guys were aware of this before they took over the place and had a special reverence for its past. It seems being British would require that. It would appear that the Beatles revived many of these centuries old traditions that once permeated the dwelling—romance, parties, esteemed guests, battles, cutting-edge fashion, decadence, raucous pulp fodder, non-stop entertainment, outrageous characters, and most noticeably when it came to money: "We'll have a good laugh spending it while we're here!"

Apple Corps purchased 3 Savile Row on June 22, 1968, for £500,000.

Apple opened its doors on July 15, 1968 with forty people following an extensive restoration.

Apple Studio closed down for good on 16 May, 1975.

Apple sold the lease at 3 Savile Row in October 1976.

It remained unoccupied until 1982.

Today, one could conceive its worth to be in the area of $40 million.

FOURTH FLOOR

BUILDING PRESSURE

During my time at Apple Records, I had the good fortune to attend various Beatle recording sessions, but going to their sessions was a little different than most. Even though I was among the fortunate few who were privileged to attend, usually we were never actually in the studio with them. When you were invited to attend one of these happenings, it basically consisted of hanging out in the halls and the lobby of the studio where they were recording. Occasionally one of them would come out on a break or hang out with us for a while. You could hear the muffled music grow louder and clearer in the few seconds the doors were open as someone went in or out. Even though we were on the outside, it felt like an elite event especially when the fans saw us entering and leaving the heavily guarded entrance to the studio.

This was not the case during the latter part of the *Let It Be* sessions. Because the studio was downstairs in the basement of the Apple building, the Beatles, Glyn Johns, George Martin, et al. would more or less merge into the studio from within the building, or make a direct beeline from a car to the stairs located to the left of the main entrance that led to the basement and into the studio. As a result, moving from

Twickenham Film Studios' dreary setting where they were originally recording *Let It Be* offered a significant shift in atmosphere to one that was lot more relaxed, natural, and conducive to a creative mind-set. The most common comment by the Beatles about working in a sound stage at Twickenham was that the atmosphere was cold. I find that not surprising as the building was originally built on the site of an old ice-skating rink.

One day George came up from the studio to Apple president Ron Kass's first floor office where Ron and I were having a meeting and interrupted with a question about a personal business matter. Although the matter at hand was neither of great import nor deeply personal, I was surprised by how openly they were discussing this subject in my presence. After Ron and George had their brief chat George apologized for the interruption and quietly made his way to the door. Then he stopped, turned in the doorway and asked if I would like to come down to the session. I looked at Kass—he looked at his watch, nodded, and said, "Why don't you go ahead? I've got a lot to do." I think I saw a subtle nod and wink exchange between them. I know how Ron Kass thought and did things, and I felt he always treated me special. Looking back, I'm convinced that he had prearranged the interruption and George's follow up invitation with all four of the "lads." It was an experience that he wanted me to have, and George was the soft-spoken messenger.

The day I was invited into the *Let It Be* sessions at Apple was second only to the concert on the roof when it comes to experiencing Rock 'n' Roll history in the making. (I had been with them in concerts at the Hollywood Bowl and Dodger Stadium in LA, in the studio with Ringo and George Martin somewhere on the outskirts of London, with George in Hollywood when he was mastering the *"White Album"* at Armin Steiner's Sound Labs and also at A&M Studios while he was overdubbing and cleaning up The Concert for Bangladesh, but this was a whole different thing!) I was blown away by being one of only two people in the studio besides the Beatles and Yoko—not the lobby, not the lounge, not the control room with the production/engineering team, but sitting on the floor in the actual recording studio while the four Beatles were recording live. Through this experience I was given the gift of understanding the essence of this very special four-piece band. The other person in the room that day was my friend Billy Preston.

The Beatles took the approach of recording the songs from beginning to end in the studio. Writing, arranging, rehearsing, recording, and accepting final takes were one continuous process. A song would grow from inception to the point where one of them would turn around and look toward the booth for George Martin's approval and then say, "Let's hear that one." If they liked it, then that was a possible album master. The idea was to have "live" takes. Looking back, I find it ironic that the album from these sessions, which was issued more than one year later, featured music that was anything but "live." It wasn't until the Apple-approved, McCartney-mandated do over *Let It Be...Naked* CD arrived more than thirty years later that the intended "bare bones" approach to the music was finally heard.

I will never forget hearing the newly released "Naked" version for the first time. It was a Christmas present from my kids shortly after its release. Decades had passed since I'd sat on that studio floor, leaning against the wall in the Apple basement, hearing the delightful rawness of this fabulous band; I couldn't believe I had forgotten how incredible the intent and concept of the original recordings had been. I was taken aback by my reaction, surprised to find myself wiping tears from my eyes as I was taken back to that time. Those days and those sounds flooded over me in a dreamy retroactive rush as I began remembering what it was all like back then.

The jagged expressions that lived in the original sessions came alive and I was so glad that others would finally get to hear what it was really all about when the greatest rock band of all time was getting back to where they once truly belonged. I miss who we were and our innocence; I miss that special time and the music that was so possible then. I especially miss them when they were...them.

I never realized how good the Beatles were until I was in the Apple basement studio, watching them play their instruments and seeing their creative process unfold before me. Everyone was, as they would say in Nashville, "a really great picker." I was especially impressed with Ringo—he was the perfect drummer for this special band. He laid it right in the pocket every time and knew how to weave his rhythms in and out of the songs in support of the raw intricacies of his band mates. In simplistic terms, he knew how to pump up the dynamics or stay out of the way when it was appropriate—the true sign of a confident, professional drummer.

Paul had the appearance of an eternal force, pushing the band all the time; John's genius would surface and everyone knew when to fall behind this expression; George seemed a little laid back, in a way distant or even disconnected, and then would, like everything else in his life, present his unique style into the mix of creative musical Liverpudlian stew. With head bowed he would blaze forth with electronics seething and screaming, and it always felt right on (to me)—like righteous sonic anger. Then he would drop back as if waiting for a response.

This sonic anger was a release of built up tension that was stemming from a lot of peripheral matters and shared by everyone in the group. Paul was resentful of the fact that he was put in a position where he was sometimes driving the band into activity and, in a way, he was forced to become an unpopular de-facto leader after Brian Epstein's death. The Beatles, and Paul in particular, typically had a strong 9-to-5 work ethic throughout their career. They saw going to the studio and creating music as their job. For the most part, that was easy because the end result was magic almost every time. But given how painful the anxiety-filled *"White Album"* sessions had been, it's easy to look back now and see how they might have been a little gun-shy about getting back in that saddle so soon.

It's no secret that one reason behind some of the hostility was the feeling that Yoko Ono was encroaching on the band's sanctity with her constant presence (even following John into the bathroom), her self-important attitude, and her unsolicited opinions, which only served to increase the discontent within the band. And let's be honest—Paul, George, and Ringo were understandably very discomfited by a strong and intrusive female presence in the room.

There were other contributing factors as well. George was getting tired of Paul "bossing" the group around and "preaching" to him specifically about his playing, plus he was sensing negative vibes from John and Yoko. On January 10, it came to a head for George. He'd had it, and the quiet one abruptly quit, calmly telling John, "I'm leaving the band now." As he headed towards the exit, he advised the others to "Get a replacement and write the NME [New Musical Express] and get a few people." George was eventually talked into coming back when the group agreed to move the sessions from Twickenham Film Studios to the newly constructed studio in the basement of their Savile Row headquarters.

It wasn't the first time a Beatle had quit the group. At one point during the recording of the *"White Album,"* Ringo was feeling out of sorts and he too made a dramatic exit. He recalled he wasn't playing his best and felt like the odd man out—as if the other three were getting on with each other, and he wasn't. He decided he couldn't take it and in late August 1968, after an inharmonious session for "Back in the USSR," he decided not to come back the next day. Ringo then flew to Sardinia in Southern Italy where he spent the next two weeks resting and recuperating. While there he spent time on the water, relaxing aboard Peter Sellers' yacht. His Mediterranean surroundings had a healing effect and even inspired him to write "Octopus's Garden," which later appeared on Abbey Road. It wasn't long before he received a telegram from his band mates telling him that he was "the greatest Rock 'n' Roll drummer in the world" and to please come back to London. When he finally walked through the studio doors, he was greeted with flowers everywhere, along with his drum kit. All was well in Beatle land for the time being, but I'm sure those pangs of insecurity still lingered for Ringo on *Let It Be.*

In addition to George and Ringo's frustrations, John and Paul had a serious communication breakdown. For some time, they had been writing songs separately, and their headspace was not functioning as one, as it had in days of old. Yoko was pretty much all John thought about, and as the old saying goes, "Four's company and five's a crowd." To Paul's credit, he gave John a long leash, making allowances for the fact that his musical partner was deeply in love. To his credit, Paul Mc-Cartney never criticized John Lennon in my presence. I have a perfect example of the depth of the loyalty they had built between each other over the years which clearly demonstrates this…

It was August 1968, and when I saw the picture for the *Two Virgins* album jacket for the first time. It was our first formal Apple gathering and included all four Beatles and the executive hierarchy of both Capitol and Apple; we were having a scheduling meeting concerning the product launch of Apple Records in America. As the Beatles' newly selected US Manager of Apple Records, my responsibility was enormous and everything I did at that time was under a microscope. The meetings were long, and, during a break, I left the group with Mal and Neil for a few minutes of attitude adjustment and medicinal tension relief. I had just returned to the meeting and sat down on the couch with John and

Yoko. John quietly leaned over, put his hand on my shoulder, placed a packet of photos on my lap, and asked me to "check 'em out."

I pulled a small batch of 8 x 10s out of the envelope and went into executive shock. "Just keep it together, the Beatles are 50 percent of Capitol's business," had been Stanley Gortikov's admonition as we boarded the plane in LA and this little travel-time nicety was still ringing loudly in my ears. I became transfixed, staring at a bunch of nude pictures of John and Yoko. I panicked because I didn't really know John very well at that time and was afraid that maybe he was making some kind of perverted sexual move on me involving his mate, and I didn't know how to respond. This was my first trip to London so I didn't know exactly what to expect and, quite frankly, was really caught off guard with his casual submission of frontal nudity. Following what I worried could be John's lead was totally out of the question, but being so focused on "keeping it together" made me very sensitive to possibly offending him through rejection and thereby losing my job. The wheels were spinning at warp speed in my head. I suddenly became acutely aware that I was just a simple, inexperienced young man in a strange foreign place. I didn't have a clue as to the ground rules in matters such as these. I certainly wasn't equipped to handle this. I guess my reaction was fairly noticeable because when I looked up in desperation toward Stanley for help, Paul started laughing and came to my rescue.

While Mal, Neil, and I were out of the room having a smoke, John brought up the subject of his desired approach for the *Two Virgins* artwork and had shown the nude photographs to everyone in the room. I had missed John's presentation, though Mal and Neil already knew about it, which meant I was the only person in the room who didn't and was shown these pictures without any preparation. Paul picked up on my dilemma, and, after letting me sweat it out for a little while, finally decided to interrupt my imagined fall from corporate and mop-top grace and filled me in on what transpired while I was out of the room. I thanked him later (in private) and I asked him (also in private) what he thought about the nude photos bit. He responded that he was totally with John in the matter. He didn't understand John's thinking but figured John was intellectually ahead of him in this area and that he would just have to catch up. He said he was sure at some point that he would catch up, and then he would be in complete agreement with John. This is what I am referring to when it came to John and Paul's loyalty to one another.

However, during the *Let It Be* sessions things were not always cute mop-top and Kumbaya time with the whole band—George and Ringo were not the only ones who recently either wanted to abandon ship or were having trouble getting uncomfortable matters sorted out. Another side issue and additional reason for the tension during these rehearsal sessions was Paul's singular idea to use footage from the rehearsals as part of a TV special or a full-length feature film he had in mind. George felt it was too much stuff to deal with all at one time…project piled on top of project. John's energies were divided between the sessions, Yoko, and apparent addiction.

So, it appears that everybody came to the *Let It Be* project with different mindsets. I felt Ringo took his place behind his kit and, for the most part, "followed the leader" and just played his part as the drummer. I noticed during the sessions I attended that he seemed to take the laid-back attitude that he was simply working a shift at his day job. Several times I spotted him looking at his watch to see if it was time to go home to his family. When it did come time to wrap things up, without a word he was off the stool and out the door. I had been to his estate in Esher Surrey and knew why he wanted to be there. It was relaxed and Zak, Jason, and Maureen were waiting for dad to come home.

In a way, observing Ringo's departure from the sessions was demonstrative of how things had changed for the four long-time friends. Poetically, it was off to the four winds with them when the day was done, as their individuality had now become so predominate that their personal lives and aspirations were no longer centered on the band. It was a natural evolution after so many years…yes, the band may have been gone but we all knew that the bond would live on.

THE CALM AFTER THE STORM

When George returned to the sessions after his departure at Twicken-ham, he had conditions—mainly that the sessions shift to Apple's studio. He was very adamant about wanting to can the TV/film idea and return to just working on the album without making the project so complicated. He also made it known that he felt the previous working plan of piling project upon project was the reason all four of them were at each other's throats in some combination or form.

Another significant change in the sessions was the addition of Billy Preston, who was invited by George to drop by Apple. Because the Beatles came from very simple working-class beginnings, they inherently possessed very good manners. One of the first things I noticed about the band when I worked with them in 1965 was how courteous they were to me and that it was natural, not a put on or a show. And, George felt that with Billy there as a guest it was hard for them to bicker and fight. When Billy sat down at the electric piano, there was also a gigantic vibe improvement in the room. (Nice call, George.) The fact that I was also there and was the guy running their company in America may have added credence to his idea that the guys would be more courteous with other friends in the room.

Before this, when George made his decision to take a step back from all the dissension that was going down in the studio, he saw in the papers that the legendary Ray Charles was performing in concert nearby at London's Royal Festival Hall. He and Eric Clapton went to the show and, to his surprise, there's his old friend Billy Preston up on stage playing in the band. He sent Billy a note backstage to reconnect. When *Let It Be* got underway, he got the idea to invite Billy to come over to the Apple studio and jam for old time's sake, thinking maybe that might break the tension.

George took on the responsibility for wrapping up the tedious task of mastering the *"White Album"* (officially titled *the Beatles*), and because I was involved in the process, I was very aware how fried he was over that never-ending project. It was roughly three months prior to these contentious *Let It Be* sessions, and once again he was definitely not having fun being in the world's biggest rock band anymore. He made the comment to me that completing a double album project had become extremely stressful and overwhelming.

After the *"White Album"* sessions were completed, he left London prior to the running order of the songs being determined. He came to LA to work on Jackie Lomax's album *Is This What You Want?* During a break from the Lomax sessions, he dropped by the Capitol Tower to listen to Capitol's acetates and did not like what he heard. He insisted that he be allowed to work with Capitol's engineers to re-master the album. Capitol destroyed thirty-three sets of lacquers that were going to be used to press the album. New lacquers were cut with the new mastering instructions developed by George and the engineers. Had he not intervened, the album would have sounded much more compressed in America.

The re-mastering session was very peaceful and laid back, with occasional fellow local artist friends dropping by Sound Recorders, a small Hollywood studio he had chosen for the re-mastering, to chat, burn one, listen to the music or just hang out. (Sound Recorders Studios was a somewhat plain, bare bones Hollywood studio owned by legendary sound engineer Armin Steiner who was known for the integrity of his facility and precise recording standards. It was located at 6226 Yucca, a side street behind the Capitol Tower. Armin closed Sound Recorders

Studios in 1971 and soon after opened the much bigger, state of the art, and very prestigious Sound Labs across the street.)

At that time, I had no idea who Armin was; but, years later, after leaving the corporate world to become a full-time producer, I spent years producing albums at his Sound Labs and soon understood why George wanted to work in Armin Steiner's environment. George knew what he was doing and chose to work with the best the industry had to offer. Armin's studios, although tastefully designed, were not known for aesthetics—it was all about true sound with him. George sensed that, and, as we all came to find out, it was not about the material world with him, it was about the art and it was about…the sound.

On the lighter side of life, I will never forget the day George's good friend Mama Cass breezed in and plopped down a joint as big as a three-pound Italian salami next to the console. She looked over at George and said, "Well, big boy, what are we going to do with this?" (I can't remember what we did after that!)

What I do remember is that George was tired of what was going down in London, so I feel his decision to come to LA could have been just to put some distance between him and the band for a while.

Getting back to Billy joining the Beatles rehearsals and George's idea that things would lighten up with Billy on board…there was a calm, childlike peace about Billy and that, coupled with his incredible chops, plus the fact that all the guys liked and respected him, did

I have to add this footnote and this may be the only time in my writings about the Beatles that I may disagree with another person's account of this event. In an excellent Harrison biography titled Behind the Locked Door, the author reported that the "reefer" incident happened at Zsa Zsa Gabor's house in Beverly Hills. I was at both places with George during this time, and my recollection of Mama Cass's happy time ciggie is quite clear—she came to the mastering session at the studio behind Capitol with that "log," not Zsa Zsa's house. In the author's defense and on a fellow writer's behalf, George may have recalled the incidence incorrectly to him, the where of the incidence was not important, it was the "wow" that gave it life. Also, on the author's behalf it should be noted that I was the one getting stoned…

help get the proper focus back on the project. It was an "inviting a good friend over for dinner" kind of atmosphere—a setting where everyone watched their manners.

I noticed this aspect of their character almost immediately, when I had my first encounter with them when we did their 1965 press conference in Capitol Record's Studio A in Hollywood. I could tell during that conference they were bored and found some of the questioning intrusive but remained calm and made light of things so they could get through the ordeal. George felt they would not air their dirty laundry in front of Billy and everyone would calm down and concentrate on the music and job at hand. George inviting me to be there was, in effect, his way of doubling down on this idea. Of course, I had no idea I might have been used and frankly don't care. I was there and loved it.

I admit that at times I felt they put on "a certain face" when I was with them as a group, so George's strategy concerning having Billy and me in the room during these trying times would somewhat validate that earlier suspicion. One of the main criticisms I have received in the past is that I always paint the Beatles as being such nice guys. Well, that is the overriding impression I got when I was around them, and that is what I remember, and I am glad for that.

I remember while going over a project idea at dinner with Ringo in the early 1990s in Beverly Hills, I made the comment that when we were setting up Apple I thought they always put on a special front for me when I was around, so I would see how professional they were as a businessman. This dinner was many years after our time at Apple and I felt as old friends we could get real with each other. His response was typical Ringo, who sarcastically put me in place. He got a serious look on his face, thought for a minute, then he said, "Oh, yeah, Ken, we didn't really have anything much else to do back then so we would sit around and come up with ideas how we could impress you."

I had been skillfully and Beatle-fully zonked.

As the sessions took place in front of me, the Beatles played, argued, and worked on pieces of music for days only to throw some of it out. The recording concept was unique and a pleasure to watch unfold. In the studio, lights were glaring and film cameras were rolling. In the control room, the tape was rolling all the time. The walls were stacked almost floor to ceiling with two-inch master tapes. Theoretically (I think) Glyn Johns was engineering and George Martin was producing; but, in reality, it looked like their roles were a little less defined. To an outside observer it would appear that they shared the production responsibilities for the project. I find it interesting that when the "Get Back" single was released, no producer credit was listed at all, making George Martin's official involvement a little unclear, even though he was there and he was their producer.

While all of this was going on down below in the basement studio… history was just waiting upon the roof five flights of stairs above them.

SGT. PRESTON, HOLY HEART OF THE BAND

BILLY PRESTON

The *Let It Be* sessions held very few surprises other than the Fab Four found it hard to shake off the lethargy and get their act together. The one guy who did have it together was someone I had known quite well.

Billy Preston was a Capitol artist and a real standout talent. He had a very aggressive manager who would virtually camp out at my office in the Hollywood Capitol Tower in the days/years before this time. Gene Taft was his name, and he was an in-the-trenches, in-your-face manager; nothing was ever good enough for his artist. He was the kind of manager every artist should have in his/her corner, but sometimes he could be a real pain. For example, he was critical of the way I dressed when we were doing promotions for Billy to the point of personally paying to have my suits altered so they would fit better. He would even buy appropriate ties to match my wardrobe. I guess I shouldn't complain about getting free clothing, but it did come at a cost: my bruised ego. I thought I was a pretty snazzy dresser until Gene cast his doubts and his vote concerning my apparel aptitude.

When Billy and I knew each other, I was an eager, young, rising executive in my late twenties, and he was a new and exciting upcoming artist in his late teens, with a lot of promise and a major recording contract. Now, instead of the two us sitting in my office at Capitol with Gene, we found ourselves (without Gene!) sitting in the most famous room in the musical world—which was any room the Beatles were recording in at that time. I sat there on the floor, leaning against the wall, taking in the fascinating scene playing out before me. While I was totally-transfixed on what was going on and in awe of just how good these guys (the Beatles) really were, off to my right and seated a few feet away, Billy was leaning over his keyboards, hands in his lap, with the biggest grin on his face. Every once in a while, he looked over at me with an even bigger smile and a look on his face as if to say, Wow, did you just hear that? And then he would jump in and lay some cool licks on them and I could see similar expressions on their faces.

There was something seamless concerning our artist/executive relationship. Billy was with Capitol Records during 1966 and 1967 when I was in charge of national promotion and artist relations at the label. When I was later promoted to Director of Independent labels at Capitol and then became US Manager of Apple Records, my old friend Billy joined me in London at 3 Savile Row for the *Let It Be* sessions not long after. He and I were uniquely "signed up" with Capitol and Apple at the same. As we sat there in that room, I had responsibilities with both labels and he had one foot in one and his heart in the other. Because of the personal relationship that had developed between Billy and the Beatles over the years, and because he brought so much to the table during the *Let It Be* sessions, he was given credit on their "Get Back" single. The billing was simple but monumental: "the Beatles with Billy Preston." (Although the Revolver album back cover contained a few credits for outside musicians who played on a particular song, Billy was given prominent billing on the label of a Beatles single!) It was something they had never done before, and a clear sign of their respect for him. If you think of all the incredible musicians they had worked with over the years, including Eric Clapton, Donovan, Brian Jones, and Nicky Hopkins, this offering on their part was highly unusual.

Apple Records bought out his Capitol contract, so Billy became part of the Beatles gang and a major Apple artist. Now, as two old friends, we found ourselves occupying common workspace once again. We were in a different town but still on the same team. Before Apple, Billy was a premier black artist on Capitol's R&B roster along with Lou

Rawls, Nancy Wilson, and Cannonball Adderley. The very talented and popular staff producer Steve Douglas had produced two albums with him at the label. I believe they did get along well, but it was inevitable for Billy to want to move to the prestigious and exciting new Apple label with the perfect new producer. That person was George Harrison, who got along exceptionally well with Billy.

Here is what's interesting about Apple wooing Billy away from Capitol: Billy was very popular at Capitol and we did have a lot invested in him. Despite the fact that he did not have a bona-fide hit single or album, as a company we believed in his potential. Keeping the relationship with Beatles intact though was unofficially priority number one at both corporate EMI and Capitol Records, and we bent over backward in keeping them happy. Now, I don't know what went on with the legal and contracts departments, as well as the Artist and Repertoire department, but all obstacles were overcome and Apple was cleared to buy out Billy's contract. But, because Capitol distributed Apple, in a way, we never lost him. Contracts and numbers may have changed, but regardless of which side of the pond I was on, Billy was still one of my artists. It was similar to the situation around why we were able to distribute Apple Records in the first place. Although, technically, the Beatles had enticed Billy to move to Apple, he was still a part of the Capitol/EMI group because of our distribution arrangement.

The Beatles first met sixteen-year-old Billy Preston in Germany in the early '60s when he was touring Europe with Little Richard. They really took to Billy and dedicated "A Taste of Honey" to him almost every night in Hamburg. They were quite taken with him both as a person and a musician—especially George. The two became fast friends and their lives intertwined over the years leading to a long and steadfast musical and personal relationship. In addition to the mutual musical respect between the Beatles and him, and the fact that they genuinely liked each other; there was no question that Billy brought something fresh to their music at a time when they were getting very burned out.

Back to the basement and the *Let It Be* sessions…

Billy entered the rehearsals smack dab in the middle of the intense ongoing fray and joined them on the all-important path that eventually led to that special day on the roof. I wasn't that aware of the dynamics going down with the band and the scenario surrounding Billy joining them at the time, but later it all made sense in light of the obvious tension that prevailed during the project. For me, I was just glad to see him in the studio with them, and in an odd way it made me feel like a proud parent watching their gifted child move up in the world. I also felt it deepened our camaraderie by having shared such a phenomenal experience.

I was also experiencing the sensation that, in a subtle way, Billy was being treated like a member of the band. In fact, at one point, John actually brought forth the idea of making him a member…the fifth Beatle! I wasn't there when this came down, so I don't know if Paul's response to John's idea was meant to be humorous or whether it was a serious remark of disagreement, but I was told he made a comment to the extent of: "Why would we want five Beatles if four Beatles can't get along with each other?" But the fact that this was considered at all really shows how the band felt about Billy.

There was freshness in the dissimilarities of the people brought from so many faraway places during these days, and then being thrown together in such astonishing moments had a sweet bizarreness about it. The gathering of unusual individuals every day in that building, and the incredible everyday happenings that went on there, was so natural and so out of this world at the same time.

The rooftop concert was the last time I saw Billy in person. I will always remember him in his glory, with the Beatles, smiling and adeptly performing at the keyboard, making beautiful music together.

Fast forward almost four decades…

Billy Preston passed away on June 6, 2006, in Scottsdale, Arizona.

I was living in the Sierra Nevada foothills in northern California and traveling a lot on speaking tours during the time of his illness. A mutual associate was trying to set up a visit between us, but Billy's condition had deteriorated so badly that it seemed inappropriate. In hindsight, I think I should have made more of an effort to see him early on in his illness—what a reunion that would have been. Sadly, this was not the only time that I delayed making the effort to see an old friend who was in their waning days in the desert.

Waylon Jennings was like family at one time in my life and I hesitated too long to see him during his last days. A flight from LAX to that same Arizona town was not that difficult to achieve on my part. I never went to Billy or Waylon's funerals, or that of any other celebrity or close friend I worked with over the years. Some people may disagree with that approach, but I liked remembering things as they were.

Funerals mark the end of a person's time on Earth and of course they always occur after the passing. But I now wonder if *Let It Be* was a pre-funeral rehearsal for the passing of the Beatles as an entity. Time had not run out for John, Paul, George, or Ringo at that time, but the band as we had come to know them was dying before our eyes and ears. Maybe bringing in Billy when they did was a form of putting them on life support. The Beatles were a living, breathing part of our existence, and it was definitely worth keeping what they brought to us alive.

They had one last dance in them, and it happened in one of the most unlikely places of all.

But that was classic Beatles—unexpected, unbelievable, and unlike any other band. They presented their biggest show in front of their smallest audience. Instead of blowing the roof off with their performance they saved the best for last by playing on a roof with the wind blowing their goodbye kiss to the world.

FIFTH FLOOR

ROOFER MADNESS

The *Let It Be* recordings (which were called *Get Back* at that stage) were wrapping up, and they still hadn't filmed the live footage segment that was planned for the movie's finale. Their first plan to accomplish this that I was made aware of was one where they would schedule a club somewhere and book the Beatles under a different name. This plan was based on the idea of sneaking the lads into the building in complete secrecy, so when the local patrons showed up at this small club to see a new upcoming group (maybe advertise them as the next Beatles), they would get the surprise of their lives. Imagine their reaction when the Beatles walked out on stage and did an "a la Cavern" style show. This gig would be the perfect climax for the *Let It Be* film, underscoring a triumphant return to their performing roots. Shooting footage of this event was of paramount importance to the project. Like a lot of things, this was a great concept, but as you can imagine, the idea of keeping it a secret was untenable. Word would inevitably get out before the show date, and the usual media madness would unfold in its typically chaotic form.

Then, for me, came the craziest and most short-lived idea for a concert: Mal and I had been given the brief assignment of scouting out deserts for a giant, one-time, free Beatles concert. Mal was to check The Sahara Desert and I was to look at desert locations in our southwestern United States. The idea would be to set up in the middle of nowhere, announce a date, and then invite anyone and everyone who wanted to come see the Beatles perform live—for free! It didn't take long to come to the realization that the logistics, expense, and realities of this idea were preposterous, to say the least. First of all, every kid in the world would be trekking to this location, and the mass of humanity would be overwhelming. Forget about staging, sound systems, accommodations, and travel. We joked that it was the stark reality of not having enough toilets that killed this idea.

Besides, who was going to pay for all of this? How would you like to look for an insurance underwriter for this Fab Four fiasco? We also concluded that only about half the people would return alive from this adventure. It would end up being every concert nightmare, rolled up into one and multiplied to the 10th power. The Rolling Stones' Altamont concert would look like a prayer meeting in comparison.

But this was what was happening in my small world of inclusion in the matter of live footage to be used as the climax of *Let It Be*. In addition to Mal's many assignments, and my remote solo task, here are some other ideas that had been in discussion and were being entertained as a unique location for the concert:

- A cruise ship filled with British fans…why does this image give me a sinking sensation?

- An old flour mill…if you're going to jolly old England, be sure to wear some flour in your hair!

- An orphanage/children's hospital…young lives changed forever.

- A torch lit amphitheater filled with 2,000 Arabs…a smoke-filled late-night idea from Derek Taylor's office?

- An empty 20,000-seat venue (Yoko's idea)…taking minimalism to higher levels?

- A prestigious English art museum…the perfect blend of mayhem and masterpieces.

THE ROOF · 93

- One of the Beatles' homes…hey, Maureen, guess who's coming to dinner?!

- The London Palladium…a short hop, skip, and jump away from Savile Row and just right for 2,200 of their closest friends.

- The Roundhouse in London…"Round and round and round and round…"

- The Houses of Parliament…no problem setting that up, right?

- A London pub…150 inside, 150,000 outside.

- The Cavern Club in Liverpool…get there first and be asphyxiated early.

- A Liverpool Cathedral…I wonder if Lennon thought they could draw a bigger crowd than a Jesus concert?

- A Greek island…any one will do, so take your pick; wear white.

- Mexico…taco standing room only.

- Barbados…why not? Makes as much sense as the others.

- The Virgin Islands…the irony is overwhelming.

- Bermuda…bring your own triangle.

- Ethiopia…a no brainer, especially during elections.

- The Giza Pyramids…as Harry Nilsson would say, "You need to have a point."

- The Grand Canyon…a lot of deep thought went into this one.

Paul even suggested the production might build a replica of the Roman Colosseum where the Beatles would enter with a group of lions…or women in chains. It was quickly decided that Paul also should be banned from long visits to Derek's aromatic office.

The idea that had generated the most traction was the 2,000-year-old Roman amphitheater in Tunisia, recalled Michael Lindsay-Hogg, which he claimed was taken seriously enough that someone was actually sent there to check it out and, in his words, "the Beatles were to start playing as the sun came up, and you'd see crowds flocking towards them through the day."

So, how exactly did they end up on the roof of Apple? It depends on who you ask. According to Paul it was his idea. Michael Lindsay-Hogg says he came up with the idea. Billy Preston thought it was John Lennon who had the idea. Others attribute it to Ringo Starr. Chris O'Dell thinks it may have come from a meeting she attended and a discussion between Tony Richmond and Michael Lindsay-Hogg.

There is the possibility that the idea for the rooftop concert may have evolved from Glyn Johns. The group had told him of their desire to play for the whole of London. During their lunch break on January 26, Ringo commented that they were thinking of putting a "garden" on the roof of their Savile Row building. At John's suggestion, the group went up to the roof, where, according to Glyn, he presented his idea of having them play up on the roof. While the Beatles would not be playing for the "whole" of the city, they would at least be playing for part of London.

The only person who didn't stake a claim to this idea was George, who hated these sessions, detested filming the documentary, and badly wanted out of the group. I think we can safely say this was not his brainchild.

One thing I am reasonably certain about is that going up to the roof was a last-minute solution, because I was working in the offices during that time and can't remember that idea being bandied about until shortly before the event.

Considering all those other locations was a waste of time because the Beatles were losing enthusiasm for the film project and becoming more and more resistant to exerting the extra effort to travel any distance to do a concert for just a few minutes of film footage. Psychologically, I think they felt that was the kind of thing a younger, hungrier band would do, and it's pretty obvious that they didn't see themselves in that way anymore.

As a unit, they were unmotivated, uninspired, lacked focus, and were quickly growing apart. Some, other than those in the inner circle, were afraid to say it, but they had grown lazy and couldn't get their act together. John, who had creatively and emotionally disengaged from the group by this time, brutally assessed that the post-*"White Album"* Beatles were "musically standing still."

Sadly, the early *Get Back* sessions bear this out. Many feel the source material for most of the songs was half-baked, underdeveloped, and needed some good old-fashioned woodshedding. I hesitate to pass judgment on the final product that came out of this get together, but I feel the attitudes described earlier did not result in the usual sparkle of genius we were used to experiencing from the greatest Rock 'n' Roll band of all time.

Paul McCartney quietly admitted to director Michael Lindsay-Hogg that the primary reason for the *Get Back* sessions and *Let It Be* film was to keep the Beatles together as a working unit and to keep them disciplined—no more, no less.

In hindsight, the band was clearly burned out from the making of the *"White Album."* They had written and produced thirty songs for what was to be a double album and single featuring "Hey Jude" and "Revolution." Those acrimonious sessions, which stretched from late May through mid-October 1968, were filled with internal strife and strained relations among the group. They were not only physically and emotionally grueling, but also were a sprint to the finish line in order to satisfy a November 22 release date to capitalize on the holiday shopping season. The Beatles recorded right up to the very last possible moment and every ounce of energy was squeezed out of them. Now, less than three months later, they were being asked to go to the well once more to deliver yet another album and a documentary feature film to boot.

I also believe travel to a distant location may have required them to be together for longer periods of time and, by now, they weren't really into each other that much. They had not been communicating effectively and had developed a patronizing tone when they were. Plus, there was the additional element of wives (George and Ringo had been married for years while John and Paul were practically headed down the aisle), the rumored or apparent conflicts among members, and, quite frankly, the outside creative interests some of them had. Paul was the only one who appeared to be all in, even though he may have resented his default leadership role. John and George were content for the Beatles to break up while Ringo seemed indifferent…he wanted to play drums or go home to the wife and kids.

But here's the problem, and it was a frustrating one to them in their heart of hearts: from the very beginning they were a performing, live, in-your-face rock band. Their immense fame swept them up and away from something they excelled in and loved the most—rocking out in the purest Rock 'n' Roll sense to a breathing, sweating, live audience, with a front row only a few feet away.

I can remember conversations that addressed their performance issues all the way back to the original Apple meetings. They were in the awkward position of suffering from their own colossal celebrity. John expressed it best when he said, "People have built us up so big in their minds that there is no way that we could go out on stage and live up to their expectations." *Sgt. Pepper*, their 1967 game-changing studio album, upped the ante. It was a modern leap forward for popular music with sounds that had never been heard before on vinyl (a quick listen to "Good Morning, Good Morning" or "A Day in the Life" will prove my point). A formal "live" concert tour was out of the question, no matter how many times they brought it up, but they still had the need and a desire for a live show. The Beatles wanted what every famous performing band wants when it's over, and that is to go out on top.

But they did finally do a live show while they were on top...of the world, of their industry, and their roof. They entered their concluding arena, disjointed, distracted, disenchanted, and with a great deal of trepidation; but, ironically, the exit had a much different tone. It felt good, that one more time. They captured that tag ending they needed. Almost a decade of togetherness wrapped up in forty-two minutes.

The day began without a sound check and ended with a soul check.

SET'EM UP, JO JO

There's something happening here and what it was ain't exactly clear… but it sure was noisy and odd. It was coming from up above and it had been going on for a couple of days. The wondering Apple staff, working in the offices below, was hearing thick planks normally used for scaffolding being installed on portions of the roof above, in preparation for a very special event.

The final decision had finally been made to get the finale for the *Let It Be* project over with by shooting the live concert footage on the Beatles' own roof—a roof that was not designed for this type activity. Fortunately, someone discerned the structure was not strong enough to hold heavy sound and film equipment, and most of all, a lot of people. The venue hovered directly over Peter Asher and Chris O'Dell's top floor offices, which just happened to be Apple's A&R department—a place where they were supposed to be able to listen to music and make "sound" decisions.

I know Peter; we spent many years before and after the Apple days as friends, co-corporate executives, and even competitors as producers. He had always been a quiet and thoughtful, focused man who took pride in his work and regarded his assignments seriously. I have to believe trying to operate beneath the epicenter of a strange commotion was not conducive to his way of thinking. It's no wonder he left town during this time.

Of course, schematics, stress tests, and in-depth structural analysis were not a part of the preparative decision to retrofit the flooring. Most likely the construction guidelines were based loosely on what is normally done when throwing together a small stage in a local park for a "Battle of the Bands" fest. So, what we got were big boards, laid out on the roof floor with sturdy planks and posts propping up the ceiling above the fifth floor. I did wonder what the fourth floor, where other Apple staffers occupied their workspaces, would do if the roof came crashing down on the fifth floor. There was no further bracing; so, what was going to protect them?

Once the location was settled and all four Beatles were in agreement with the time and plan, furtive activity began at 4:00 a.m. on January 30. Crews began shuffling, carting, hauling, dragging, and coaxing heavy and awkward sound, lighting, film, camera, and musical equipment, as well as running a mile of audio cable up five floors from the basement studio to the rooftop. This was no small feat given that, in order to get to the roof, everything had to be brought up the final steps to the roof by either going up a ladder or narrow rickety stairs. Trying to hoof Billy Preston's Fender Rhodes Seventy-Three keyboard and Fender Twin Reverb amps up there was just not going to happen under those conditions. It didn't matter if it was a ladder, narrow rickety stairs, elevator, or state-of-the-art escalator, Billy's stuff simply wouldn't fit around a bend in the staircase or through the door. In order to get the Fender Rhodes topside, staffers had to hoist it through a skylight that had to be completely disassembled and then put back together afterward.

There were other improvisations made as well: sound engineer Alan Parsons was sent out to buy ladies stockings to shield the harsh January wind from blowing into the microphones. Alan recollected to Guitar Player magazine years later, "I walked into this department store and said, 'I need three pairs of pantyhose. It doesn't matter what size.' They thought I was either a bank robber or a cross-dresser."

Meanwhile five stories and a basement below, the audio portion of the concert was recorded on two eight-track recordings in Apple's studio...yes, in the basement. The session was engineered down there with

Glyn Johns monitoring the multi-track recordings and talking to Alan and the band occasionally through an intercom. Alan was a healthy young man but also very tall, so picture him running up and down the vertical length of the building, and possibly doing a bit of ducking at strategic points along the way.

On a gentler note, George Martin was also present in the bottom room, but his was a curious role on *Let It Be*. He was asked to be the supervising producer and instructed by John Lennon that "none of your production rubbish" was needed for this project. That may have sounded a bit harsh coming from John to a gentle man he deeply respected, but John had this manner at times that could be very off putting until you got a better grasp on his nature. It was actually one of the great things about him in that he would cut through the mental clutter, which simplified discussions so you didn't have to ask twice about what he was thinking.

I wish I had this understanding one day in early 1969 when John and Yoko had called me into their ground floor office and were raking me over the coals after presenting me with "The King of Fuh," a record by an American singer who called himself Brute Force. They sat shoulder to shoulder behind one long desk that dominated the whole end of the room. My chair seemed smaller than most and, to this day, I'm convinced that they had the legs shortened so their guests would feel even smaller than they already did in their presence. John wanted me to take the record back to America and put it on the Apple release schedule there, and the purpose of our meeting was because he wanted me to explain my negative position on both the "King of Fuh" record and his impassioned request to include it on an upcoming singles release schedule in the US

Unfortunately, the song's lyrics, due to creative repositioning, were so blatantly objectionable by American standards that Capitol Records couldn't release that record in the US on Apple, or any other label, even if they wanted to. It would be a "brown paper bag, under the counter" type of thing at best, as I tried to tell them.

Then they started in on me: "We thought you were one of us, Ken… but it looks like you are just one of the establishment, like everyone else. We thought we could trust you of all people to understand the concept behind the whole Apple enterprise. I didn't know we brought you over here from the 'land of the free' to act as Apple's personal tight-assed censor!"

Mere words can't explain how intimidating they were. From a cowering position in that condensed chair it was difficult to command stature, but once again I attempted to explain it had nothing to do with me or Stanley Gortikov or Capitol Records or any of our personal beliefs. It had to do with those pesky FCC regulations, other legalities, and the like. As hard as I tried, I never quite got the sense that, in this particular matter, I totally convinced them that I was indeed "one of them."

Looking back over the "King of Fuh" lyric debate really makes it easy to now see the separate worlds we lived in and how times have changed since then. Today I doubt anyone would even comment on the record's textual immorality or, for that matter, question the visual propriety of the jaw-dropping *Two Virgins* album cover. I remember I walked out of their office that day devastated, but now I understand that they were looking to me to fight some of their battles in America—battles against the suits and what John considered a rigid and out of date way of thinking that stymied his creative efforts. Over time, this was just one of many one-sided exchanges between us, some of which would come into the communication center at Capitol via transatlantic cable and be delivered to my office by a blushing secretary who had to receive and relay the profanity-laced messages.

Many years later, long after my Apple days, I was in London having lunch with Ron Kass and Neil Aspinall about recreating Apple with the original crew. We were also reminiscing about the good old days and our individual experiences with the Beatles. I told him how fortunate I felt to have been able to spend personal time and become friends with each one over the years, except for John. I told Ron I felt John didn't really like me because he was so caustic with me at times. Kass gave me a very surprised look when I told him that. "That's odd," he said, "because John was the one who liked you best!" It turns out, according to Kass, that John felt comfortable around me because he trusted me and felt he could say what was on his mind. I only wish I had known that twenty or so years earlier.

The ultimate irony here, going back to John's comment to George Martin concerning producing the *Let It Be* sessions, is that when the group was breaking up, John Lennon tapped Phil Spector to come in and "salvage" the album. Most of us feel he actually "savaged" the album! Well, Spector being Spector used every production trick in the book to get the album to shimmer. It was far from the raw and unadorned sound the Beatles had in mind for *Let It Be*—or, as George Martin once joked, that the credit on the album jacket should have read, "Produced by George Martin, over-produced by Phil Spector."

The one person who appeared to live up to their billing as director was Michael Lindsay-Hogg. Michael performed admirably and professionally throughout the shoot under a difficult set of circumstances. Imagine the position he was in and the task before him: he had to witness the group imploding before his very eyes, and he had to record it for posterity.

For the performance, he set up close to a dozen cameras positioned in several locations, to give the one-time event a wide range of coverage. He strategically placed cameras on the roof, nearby rooftops, in the windows of 3 Savile Row and in the street to record the reaction of onlookers. He even placed one in the Apple reception area to capture the inevitable moment when the London police would knock on the front door and tell the Beatles to "knock it off."

Everything came together quickly, and by lunchtime it was a go. The stage was constructed, the instruments were warmed up, the PA system was rigged, the cameramen were in place, and the engineers were eagerly waiting to push the record button. All the Beatles had to do was show up and play. The question on everyone's mind was, "Could the Beatles be the Beatles one more time?"

I could never figure out how I was so unaware of the decision to perform on the roof, and so oblivious to the fact that it was so frantically being made ready for the performance. I was probably using an office on a lower floor where the construction and movement wasn't so obvious. I imagine whatever I did hear I simply assumed was someone having their office remodeled or that they were still converting spaces, which was not that unusual. Logically, I would use George's office to work because when he was in LA he would use a corner of my eighth-floor office in the Capitol Tower to make phone calls, hang out, or hide out when he had down time between appointments. His office at Apple was on the ground floor and kind of off by itself, so I would be about as far away from the roof as you could get in the building. I don't believe he spent that much time there, so it was a convenient trade off. As my times there were brief and sporadic, I had no place to call my own, so most other times I would be found in Ron Kass's or Derek Taylor's office or wandering about looking for an unoccupied space. Things were that casual, and I was never made to feel like I was invading anyone's domain.

But, if they involved me when I was thousands of miles away by asking me to look for a location on another continent, why wasn't I clued in when I was just down the hall and the event was imminent? No matter; I turned out to be one of the chosen few to witness history being made up close on the roof.

Of course, if I was looking for logic I was in the wrong building.

THE ROOF

A DAY ON THE ROOF

"HEY, WE ARE GOING UP ON THE ROOF."

Ilooked up from my borrowed desk in one of the Apple offices to find Mal Evans looming over me. (Even when he was at my side, Mal's gentle-giant countenance made me feel like, as always, he had me covered.)

We had become close friends in a very short time, and he had that look on his face that said he was going to share something special with me. Mal was very childlike to those who knew him and his invitation was akin to the way kids want to share something really cool with their pals. He and I developed a special bond that began the first day we met and lasted, unbroken, right up until a troubled phone call he placed to me virtually minutes before his death on that terrible night in 1976, when the police shot him to keep him from hurting himself.

I always had the feeling that, in addition to taking care of the Beatles, Mal gathered me in like a mother hen and included me in his realm of responsibility. I do know this: the reason I had such a great and warm acceptance with the guys from the get-go was because of Mal's immediate blessing. They trusted him, he trusted me and…it was that simple. In those days, you didn't get anywhere near the Beatles unless you first passed muster with Mal or Neil. Thanks to Mal, I was invited into one of the inner circles that allowed me to share in many fascinating Apple and Beatles moments.

If I had to single out one event that stood out above all the others during the time I was in the music industry and working with the Beatles, it would by far be their last "concert." That wild and impromptu event presented the end of a time warp, an intimate gathering, a worldwide event, and a moment like no other. It took place during the punishing cold midday of Thursday, January 30, 1969, and warmed our hearts. The fact that I ended up becoming a small part of the historical musical phenomenon called the Beatles began with being in the right place at the right time. The fact that I was working at Apple in London when this event took place is probably the penultimate example of good fortune in my entertainment business life.

"What do you mean we're going up to the roof?" I responded, knowing that Mal's demeanor meant something exciting was getting ready to take place. That's when he told me that at 1:00 p.m. our live footage for the *Let It Be* film was going to take place just steps away. Because things that happened at Apple always seemed so otherworldly, his buoyant enthusiasm filled me with childlike anticipation. The noise and unusual physical activity that had been permeating the building for the past couple of days made sense and everything came into focus. Our previous mutual scouting assignments to look for a rock concert location in the Sahara or Sonoran Desert had boiled down to this day and time in Rock 'n' Roll space. I had been given a heads-up shortly before "show time," and on his command, I headed up the stairs and became a part of "the Roof."

The roof was a last minute and rational solution to getting live footage for the film. It was definitely the most cost-effective idea and proved to be very efficient when considering the raw effort needed on everyone's part. Apple staffers, stage crews, and carpenters readied the roof surface and the filming and recording electronics. It was an actual gig and there were no complicated logistics, no hotels, airfares, no per diem, no out of control food bills, and…no unions to deal with. Everybody just came to work that day. There was a time and a place and a band. There was no advance publicity, but we definitely ended up with an audience.

As zero hour neared, Mal locked the downstairs doors and staffers, stagers, and stars alike all became willing prisoners of an exciting blend of history and music that wonderful day at 3 Savile Row. A sense of calm mixed with anticipation filled the air once the doors were locked and there was no doubt that it was a go. We were just like kids playing with things much larger than we understood.

There were just a few of us up there and it felt good—it was personal; it was special—and we got to witness a gathering of Rock 'n' Roll angels expecting to fly. Words and music soon soared out of the very heart of the staid Mayfair financial district and into the ears and souls of the unsuspecting people on the streets. London was the center of cutting-edge music, and in the neighboring buildings of this vibrant city, secretaries, bankers, wool merchants, and deliverymen alike were jolted alive by the rockin' that was rollin' off the Apple rooftop. Everyone within a mile of that place will proudly state for the rest of their lives that they were there the day the music came wafting down the streets, echoing and slamming up against the red brick buildings. Melodies and rim shots blew in through the cracks and into board meetings, while Lords and loonies alike stood frozen along Savile Row, necks craned upward to the rooftops. They immediately knew who it was—they were just trying to work out what was happening. These were not the usual sounds coming down the roads of London's sedate financial district at lunchtime.

Soon the streets and sidewalks were clogged by voluntary standstill, open windows started dotting the sides of the once sealed buildings, and bodies began lining the ledges of the adjoining structures. It was all so unexplainable, yet so incredibly wonderful.

It is the simpler events that took place inside this day that I remember the most. The "lunchtime" show time had been set, and all the Beatles were in the building, ready to go on stage at that time. I walked into the office they were using as a spur of the moment holding room to give a message to John, and found before me a young group of rockers going over their set while showing signs of nervousness and pre-stage jitters, just like any other band. When it was time, they came out of this space and filed out through the door onto the roof stage, just like so many groups I had seen heading into a performance a thousand times. There is that unique moment for entertainers when they are told "It's time," and they make the journey along that strange distance from a dressing room to the stage. This time it was by way of a narrow staircase. Until a band knows they have connected with an audience, there is that deep down indescribable fear of not pulling it off, no matter who you are. (Andy Williams once told me that even after decades of mega success and thousands of concerts, he never stopped wanting to throw up just before he went on stage.) Football players experience it until they have had their first physical contact on the field—at which point they are finally in the game.

Well, that day, an up-close audience and one out of sight in the distance, felt a connection—a connection to something so unique and special that they still hold it dear to this day. I know the Beatles felt it too, and were gifted in return by performing their biggest concert for just a few people. They were able to hear and sense each one in the rarified air of their own space.

I later realized that what I perceived as nervous anticipation had more to do with personal concerns way beyond my understanding. The rules of their game had changed somewhere along the way—confused and un-amused, the players decided they would play just this one more time—a whole note…a final chord.

The Beatles walked through the door and out onto that cold roof to a makeshift stage and performed their last live concert.

Outside of Michael Lindsay-Hogg's film crew, the sound people (which included Alan Parsons, Glyn John's recording assistant), and noted photographer Ethan Russell, the only directly associated people in the immediate 12 x 15 square foot area on the roof that day consisted of the four band members, keyboardist Billy Preston, a few Apple staffers, Mal Evans, Ron Kass, Jack Oliver, Peter Brown, Beatles' equipment manager Kevin Harrington, plus four audience members. (A more complete list of people who were there will be included in a later chapter) There was only one bench brought up to the roof for "the audience"—four people who were privileged to be sitting just a few feet away and to the left of the Beatles. From left to right were Yoko Ono, Maureen Starkey, myself, and Chris O'Dell. We were the "audience," so in essence it was a sold-out concert…and all four seats were comped! (Ron Kass's wife Anita joined Ron on the roof once the music began, so she was technically in the standing room only section.)

None of us four had any real work to do while we were on the roof that day, so the only thing we qualified for was to listen. (I had work to do downstairs, but I was on a lunch break I guess you could say!) We huddled together trying to stay warm and out of the cold wind.

The chimney at our backs suggested warmth, but it offered none, so all the huddling had to do, with the four of us using it as a windbreaker. Maureen and I were the lucky ones in the middle. The way I see it, I was the luckier of the two of us because I was also next to another very attractive young lady: Chris O'Dell. In the most famous of the roof top pictures, Kevin Harrington can also be seen kneeling in front of John Lennon while holding a clipboard with the words for "Dig a Pony" for him to read. I now like to joke that John never would have made it on "American Idol" because he often had trouble remembering lyrics.

Mal, who was never more than a few steps away from the lads when they were together like this, was there, along with Billy Preston who would eventually be seated just off to Paul's right. Ethan Russell was the only photographer on the roof that day and he took a massive number of incredible pictures. He was a real pro and never let his presence interfere with the magic of the moment. In actuality, there were only about a dozen or so people living in the sweet spot of that historic day. (As a side note: the standing order the Beatles usually assumed on stage was different from how they were positioned on this day. John and George switched positions, which placed John in the middle to the right of George. I've never heard a reason for this change but wonder if adding Billy Preston to the lineup brought this about or, even more curiously and less likely, if it was because it had been so long since they had performed live that their current stage order was no longer automatic.)

Besides the obvious band and film equipment important for making the event function as planned, there was the wardrobe situation. Mainly the coats! For me, Mal's earlier heads up did throw me into a brief panic because I knew how cold it was down on the street that morning and imagined the temperature on the roof to be much worse. I didn't own a warm coat in southern California, but it usually wasn't that big of a problem because once I got off the plane in London I was chauffeured around and my moments outside were brief...from the limo to the hotel entrance, from the limo to the office door, or from the limo to the front of a restaurant, etc. Fortunately, I had just enough time to borrow someone's coat at the office, run out to the street, and go into the first place I saw that sold clothes. I found a white topcoat on sale, bought it, had them throw it in a bag without really checking it out and ran back to the office. Unfortunately, it turned out to be an unlined rubberized raincoat. When I put it on and walked out onto the roof a short time later it became frozen stiff and offered almost no protection from the cold. I could have taken it off and stood it up in the corner. But the unintended cool thing was that, with it being white, I am easy to spot in Ethan's pictures and Michael's film because I was "the guy in the white coat" floating about in a sea of black attire.

I was a total southern Californian who hadn't experienced a real winter in many years and hated it when the weather started dipping down into the low-sixties. But on that magical day you could have put me in my shorts and hosed me down with ice water and I wouldn't have left this "happening" on the roof for all the money in the world.

The day began bitterly cold and windy, and it was about 45 degrees in metropolitan London at show time, so you can imagine how cold it must have been five stories up—especially because at that elevation the band had nothing to shield them from the punishing wind. (I don't remember the words "wind chill factor" being used in weather forecasts in those days, but in today's news it could have been reported as deep into the 30s.) To make matters worse, fog was looming and rain was threatening the shoot. These and other limiting factors ruled out going through with an earlier idea of hiring a helicopter for aerial footage. That would have provided some fascinating footage, but was a very expensive and complex proposition to consider, especially with the predictably uncooperative nature of weather.

For a while I stood a few feet from George with four lit cigarettes between my fingers, so he could reach over and warm the tips of his fingers. John also complained that he had trouble making the chords because his left hand was so cold. I was under the impression he borrowed Yoko's fur coat to keep him warm while Ringo had commandeered Maureen's bright red raincoat, but there are pictures of John wearing that coat on other occasions while Yoko was wearing a black coat. And then there are pictures of Yoko wearing that same coat with John wearing a black coat. It may technically have been her coat, but I have a feeling that they just shared those two items. I didn't see him come into the building that day, so I don't know if he swapped coats with her before going up to the roof. I do remember she was wearing a black coat as she sat with us by the chimney. I never thought about it, but I wonder if the ladies were stuck with inferior protection from the cold. I can't remember or tell from the pictures exactly what Maureen was wearing. I do know, by looking at that picture of the four of us up there that day, that we were, as already mentioned, "huddling from the cold."

I am going to stay general in describing the police portion of the event because I was locked into position on the roof itself with limited perspective, but I feel the press coverage was a bit off the mark and overblown. If you go by some reports, the impression would be that the big bad police marched into the building, stormed up the stairs, and burst out on the roof with billy clubs drawn. From my observation point, and the accounts of others on the scene, that description is a bit more dramatic than what actually happened. Savile Row was a rather proper area known for its banking institutions and high-end tailors. The Apple building and the Westminster police station were within shouting distance of each other. Of course, the bankers were there first and obviously had more pull with the "Blue Meanies" than the long hairs, and it only took one highly-influential and connected bank executive along with a neighboring wool merchant to insist that the intolerable situation soaring above and blowing down the Row be resolved posthaste. I do believe the Bobbies arrived at the front door with a full head of steam, and when Apple staffers originally denied entrance there was a threatening exchange from the authorities. I liked it that Michael Lindsay-Hogg (I believe Mal was also involved with this) had the foresight to have cameras installed at the entrance ahead of time—everyone was sure they would be paying a visit.

If you knew dear gentle giant Mal, it would be easy to understand that when he came down to the entrance, relieved secretary Barbara O'Donnell from guard duty (she was obediently following Peter Brown's instruction to hold off the police as long as she could), and talked to them that the situation mellowed out. It didn't take long for the Bobbies and their new buddy Mal to work out a plan as they pondered the situation together on the first floor. Mal told me that, because the police were so excited to be part of the scene, when they finally understood what was happening, they worked in concert with him and coordinated the timing for when they would be allowed to shut the thing down. I guess you could say there were two concerts on the roof that day.

In many areas of the Beatles' lives, Mal and Neil shared identical responsibilities, so it would typically be either Neil or Mal who would have confronted the Gendarmes at the door. I do believe, because of the difference in their personalities, that it was a good thing that Neil was off having his tonsils removed and Mal was in charge of the encounter. Neil was a little rougher around the edges—known for his acid-tongue—and would have most likely been a little sterner, maybe even abrasive, in the way the matter was handled. Both Neil and Mal would have taken a bullet for the lads and were extremely protective of all things Beatles at all times. When it came to their bosses' well-being, their actions and motives were always above reproach.

My impression was that the police were really having a fun time with it all. In fact, to show how "with it" and cool they were, someone from the station actually called ahead before coming over to "raid" the building. This gave everyone a ten-minute heads-up in which to dump whatever "stash" they had with them. Also, in at least one of the pictures taken that day by Ethan Russell, you can see an officer standing with Mal, waiting before the plug was pulled. They both look pretty relaxed to me.

As they began their journey up the stairs and through the building I was told toilets flushed in unison up and down all five floors—everyone waited until they knew for sure the police were coming before "cleaning house." I couldn't hear the waterworks from the roof, but I bet it sounded like Niagara Falls when the police were coming up the stairs. Anyway, there were no arrests when they got to the roof, but it would have added a nice touch to the film to have them shut the band down while they were playing and have the four lads cuffed and commandeered off the roof and carted away in a paddy wagon. That might have been great for TV, but the potential outcome could have been bad for the band. There was a chance that a judge may have not possessed the same sense of humor, and the Beatles would end up with a "rap sheet."

As you can imagine, things were happening pretty fast up there; but, in a way, the police situation was handled in such a manner that it turned into cleverly organized moments of chaos. It wasn't as though, in the midst of all this, the Beatles had a ten-second band meeting, or Apple staffers who were present at the time briefly gathered together and voted on how to choreograph the moves to get the most mileage out of the situation. No one asked me how this would play in America if we mixed a little arrest into the scenario. No one ran downstairs to check with Derek Taylor to see if he could wring a lot of publicity if they spiced up the event a bit with a few handcuffs or a bop on the head with a billy club. It was probably more like a split-second decision, where Peter Brown turned to Mal with a look, wondering if that would be cool, or, as would be expected, John might want to do something like that in defiance. I personally feel we could have gotten a lot of mileage out of that and that the fans would have loved it, plus it would have injected a lot of unintended "unplugged" pathos into the moment. But wisdom prevailed, and interestingly, when this rather monumental event came to an end it was because of the possible heavy criminal offense of being a "noise violation."

It is actually hard to call it a concert, even though there was what I have playfully called an audience—the four of us seated in front of the band. I think of it more as a performance with a purpose, backed by a few Apple staffers standing behind the band, and a working crew. Aside from that, there were the peripheral people—those watching from adjacent buildings and windows, plus a few interlopers and stragglers who had their own brief special moment before being quickly escorted away. The band wasn't visible from the sidewalks below, so the street people never got to see the show.

So, when it was over, the Beatles headed for the exit to make their way down the stairs. I watched their backs as they went through the small weathered door and it never entered my mind as I watched them go that a few marvelous minutes earlier I witnessed their final moments as a live Rock 'n' Roll band. They would be recording artists for a little while longer, but not really a functioning band anymore. I think if I would have had that realization it would have been a very dizzyingly emotional moment.

Chris and I fell in line behind Maureen and Yoko to make our way to the offices below, neither of us saying a word. Strangely, none of us talked about it that day. In fact, for the most part, none of us shared our feelings about that time until many decades later. I remember as we made our way down the stairs I had an odd empty feeling inside, devoid of thought…just emptiness. I felt like even though I brought nothing with me to that place that day, I had left something behind. No…it was more complex than that. I left a piece of me up there while, at the same time, I also took something with me. It turned out to be a deeply buried treasure that would take me years to uncover, something imperishable.

When it was over, I wanted more. I still do.

I caught an early nonstop flight the next morning out of Heathrow, and many hours later, which was my custom when flying west from London to LA, I hailed a cab at the airport and went directly to my office where I would re-enter the comparative normalcy of a remaining Hollywood day's events.

Upon my return, the first question Capitol co-worker Roger Karshner asked me when I got off the elevator was: "When did you get back?" I didn't answer, and I know my long odd smile in response may have been a little confusing to him. I left it at that. I turned, walked into my office, closed the door behind me, and sat down to what was becoming an unfamiliar desk. I looked out the window from my eighth-floor vantage point at the backside of Hollywood.

Get back?, Roger asked. After those past days, those people, that place, I began wondering if this place is where I "once belonged."

MOVING PICTURES

Michael Lindsay-Hogg was everywhere on the roof that day.

I knew that name and also knew from the first time I saw him in the Apple building that Michael Lindsay-Hogg was somewhat a legend in the making, or at least someone I should take notice of. There were a lot of characters with these intriguing names floating about the periphery of the Beatles world, and, whether Michael had just graduated from middle school or had two Oscars and a nod from the Queen, how could you ignore a name like that? I know when I inquired about who he was or what he did I was given that puzzled, askance look that only Brits can do. In my, "Hey, dude, surfs up" interpretation of all things irrelevant, this learned look meant, "Who's Michael Lindsay-Hogg? Are you daft, mate?"

Because he was a film guy, there was a certain detachment or aloofness about him when it came to this suntanned American invader into a very private world: the molten center of London's Rock 'n' Roll royalty. We never met. We never said hello. I occasionally fell within his gaze. I would look away. I must admit he was a bit occupied at the time, and each time I was around him I was basically just taking a break from my other activities in the building. Also, it must be noted that no one found any reason to introduce us even though we were fellow Americans.

I was intrigued by the way he went about things and couldn't tell if the lads were so comfortable with him that there didn't seem to be much need for chemistry or camaraderie, or if that was just his standard operational way of going about things. Of course, it's possible that it was because John, George, and Ringo were really just not into the whole idea of making a documentary. Paul, well, he was Paul. *Magical Mystery Tour* gave him a taste of filmmaking and he wanted to make this documentary an artsy and progressive work—even suggesting the open soundstage forum at Twickenham Studios, possible camera angles and tracking, and sound recording. One of Paul's strengths was that he was always going to roll up his sleeves and give it everything he had.

As far as Michael Lindsay-Hogg and Kenneth Floyd Mansfield were concerned, the whole non-thing between us had that cattlemen and sheep men kind of feel...you know, music people and film people, west coast LA and east coast New York City people—both sure within our souls that our raison d'être was much more beneficial to mankind as a whole than the other person's hopeless endeavors.

I think I liked him though, and I have a feeling that after a jaunt to a nearby pub and a couple of pints of warm brown and bitters, followed by sharing a few exaggerated exchanges of how exciting our lives within our chosen fields were, that we would have become friends. I would fly into London from the hippie capital of the world wearing moccasins or surfer sandals while his shoes were always these noticeably cool, finely-crafted European leathers. I know my lasting impression of how impressed I was with his footwear is an odd way to frame my remembrance of Michael, but imagine looking at all of this through the eyes of an Idaho-raised, California-crazed young man barely out of his twenties in this strange new world and turbulent times. It wasn't always the big things that caught my eye, but the small differences between us—the everyday aspects and disparities of our individual cultures.

Remember also this was the sixties, it was Europe, London, the Beatles...Apple. At times, I felt like an accordion player at a heavy metal Battle of the Bands competition, because things were so over-the-top cool and cutting-edge in London's rock scene.

I keep referring to things as being proper British or very English, but it was like that, much more than it is today. The milk and beer was still served warm, girls were called "birds," and when you reached for a "fag" you were getting ready to light up a cigarette. Things were very defined and different then, and the beauty of it was that it was just exactly as I expected...maybe that is what overwhelmed me. Possibly it was being immersed cold turkey into the Beatles wild, crazy world that resided within the boundaries of a sedate and staid area called the Mayfair district that was so mind boggling.

Maybe I wasn't so crazy after all in being intrigued by Michael Lindsay-Hogg—he was extremely interesting, and I sensed him being there was a cool thing. Check it out...

Michael had long suspected he was the love child and only son of one of the movie industry's most famous and wildest directors of all time: Orson Welles. Rumors surrounding this possibility were widespread, and his mother, Geraldine Fitzgerald, who was an actress (Wuthering Heights) and had worked with Welles on Broadway in the late 1930s, repeatedly discredited the whole notion. She did eventually acknowledge the truth to family friend Gloria Vanderbilt, but never told her wondering son, who was raised by Edward Lindsay-Hogg, though at arm's length. Interestingly, it seems that all along Orson Welles' oldest daughter agreed with Michael's stance on this. Great resolve for Michael came many years later when, in 2009, Gloria Vanderbilt wrote him a letter describing his mother's long and deep relationship with Welles, and verified that Welles was indeed his father.

Vanderbilt wrote, "When G (Geraldine) told you that she 'never had an affair with Orson,' it was because your 'father' was still alive, and she wanted to protect you in those years when you were coping with growing up. She did tell me that Orson was your father....The important thing now is to once and for all find peace. And I know this is what she would want for you."

Knowing this helped me realize that he did look like a bit like his dad and, in fact, sounded like him at times. As he suspected and believed, filming was in his blood, and by age twenty-four he was directing the 1964 top teen popular British rock music TV show "Ready Steady Go." Among other accomplishments he became known as a favored director of promo videos, and between 1966 and 1968 garnered great notoriety as the director of several videos for both the Rolling Stones ("Jumpin' Jack Flash" and "Child of the Moon") and the Beatles ("Paperback Writer," "Rain," "Hey Jude," and "Revolution") thus throwing him into the spotlight of his profession.

That spotlight must have been somewhat dimmed when Michael started filming the Beatles at an open stage in London's Twickenham Studios in early January 1969. As soon as he rolled tape, the camera caught the band creatively frustrated, hard feelings rising to the surface, playing poorly, and looking rather bored with it all. Most of all, the cameras caught the beginning of the world's most dynamic pop group coming apart at the seams.

The Beatles later claimed that they weren't early risers, the studio was unfamiliar and chilly, and they weren't used to the intrusive cameras, giving off a fishbowl-like vibe.

When I first watched the film, for me it failed to capture the magic of the Beatles I witnessed in the Apple studio. But I wasn't at Twickenham and I never saw all the cold discord that went on there. I do know I have never heard anyone comment about what a warm, inviting, and creativity-inspiring place it was. McCartney felt that those sessions were sabotaged by the taciturn atmosphere, and that uncomfortable feeling added to the mix of their unsteady personal dynamics. It was even further complicated by a lot of stress and even more drugs.

I entered the scene when the comfort level was greatly improved by the fact that they were at home on Savile Row and Billy Preston brought a whole new uplifting feel, as well as good music, to the table. I know, as a record producer, that when a visiting artist or a top executive from the record label entered the studio that we all, shall we say, "put our best foot forward" for the benefit of the guest. So, there we were in a friendly setting, with a personal friend, and musician they admired, plus the head of their record label in America in the room with them and what I saw and experienced was just what I thought I would see…the greatest band in the world working and focusing on a very important project.

However unproductive the Beatles felt the Twickenham sessions were, Michael shot 223 rolls of film and recorded approximately 200 songs, improvisations, jokes, new works, and a wide variety of cover tunes over a ten-day period, which amounted to about sixty hours of movie time. He had a lot to work with given the fact that *Let It Be* had a running time of eighty-one minutes.

So, it's no wonder I couldn't help but notice there was something about this guy, other than his shoes, when he showed up to direct *Let*

It Be with the Beatles. (By the way, during the '60s and '70s he directed tons of TV movies and series, and then later in the '80s, when he was in his forties, he also directed successful Broadway shows in his hometown New York City including *The Boys of Winter*, *Agnes of God*, and *Whose Life Is It Anyway?*)

But on the cold historical date of January 30, 1969, Michael Lindsay-Hogg and I, who by now were long-time strangers, were on the roof together—his attention was focused on putting the final touches to *Let It Be*, while my focus was on just trying to keep warm and irrelevant. If, by circumstance, we are ever brought together again and formally introduced, I am sure we will consider ourselves special friends because of the roof, as happened with Alan Parsons and me—and this time I'm sure we will find time to sit down, have a couple of pints of warm brown and bitters, and enjoy reminiscing about old times!

AND THE BAND PLAYED ON...

"THE 'LIVE' ROCK 'N' ROLL EVENT OF ALL TIME."
—ROLLING STONE MAGAZINE

Life can be an amazing trip when contemplating some of the amazing contradictions faced along the way, especially when trying to reconcile them in retrospect. For me, it is the juxtaposition of some of my least favorite Beatles songs and my favorite moment with them in what I consider the highlight of my career.

I have revealed a lot about the marvelous things that occurred on January 30, 1969, and the people who made it so magical, but to this point I have not mentioned one song that was performed on the roof that day. In order to take a proper look at the set list I have asked Beatle historian and good friend Brent Stoker to join me once again as we go back in time and listen to the music together. Brent was the contributing editor of my first two books; *The Beatles, the Bible, and Bodega Bay* (May 2000) and *The White Book* (October 2007) and because he knows more about "all things Beatles" than I or most other people do, I believe taking a hard look from Brent's learned point of view at the music they chose for that day is paramount. I liked most of the songs they performed but a couple didn't make my "all-time best of" list. Because for anyone to even question the supremacy of any Lennon and McCartney composition would border on blasphemy to their most fervent fans, I deem it my duty to realize that each of these songs is worthy of utmost respect. Brent's view of the music that day reads as if he had bowed in reverent remembrance of their spirited offerings.

The heart of that day wasn't just the songs, it was that particular performance that gave them their true beat. First, consider the well-known fact that the Beatles had not played together live since appearing at San Francisco's Candlestick Park on August 29, 1966 (885 days prior). To most observers this should have been a great hindrance and distraction, but for me this fact alone is what made this day so magical—what made the performance so unique and incredible. Listen to the raw tapes and consider how cold it was up there, how disjointed everything was on almost every level in their lives, the air of discomfort between them going into it, and the fact that, in a sense, they were not 100 percent united on the whole idea and maybe not really into it! But something happened; the minute it did become a live performance they became who they were—a really good band and longtime friends who had experienced things that only they could understand. Those forty-two minutes together gathered into its center everything they had known about and meant to each other for so many years. No one, not even the four of them, actually understood that this was the final encore of the greatest Rock 'n' Roll show on Earth. Everything that followed was defined by those precious minutes.

All my realizations about them and those minutes came out of a few quick glances, when Paul and John turned to one another as if to say "Yeah, this is us; this is who we have been, are right now, and always will be...a really good live band and the best of mates." When I observed this happening from only a few feet away I got chills, not from the cold, but from the warmth of those exchanges. Those instances, the ones I referred to earlier as the "simpler events," are the most treasured things I took with me from that day.

Although, before they came out through the door and onto the makeshift stage, it is interesting to note how it all began. George really didn't even want to go out there; Ringo didn't see the point; and John just took the stance of resignation by saying something like, *Hey just do it, get it over with.* I don't know how Paul felt during those final seconds, but I can almost see him smiling and saying, "Okay, show time; let's go!"

Look at some of the elements inside the presentation of those songs. Check out the relaxed banter that displayed so many of the traits that made so many fans love them. They were funny, personal, and they offered it up as if to a large, live audience, and they were also very, very Beatle-ish. For instance…

John: "We've had a request from Martin Luther." (I read somewhere this was an insider comment to do with time spent at the Cavern Club in the early days.)

John: (Later, following the Martin Luther bit) "We've had a request from Daisy, Morris, and Tommy."

Paul: (John's banter prompted quips from Paul when the bobbies began attempting to shut things down in the middle of Get Back.) "You've been playing on the roofs again, and that's no good, and you know your mummy doesn't like that / She gets angry / She's gonna have you arrested! Get back!"

John: (Of course, the most classic, most oft-repeated words are when it was all played and done.) "I'd like to say thank you on behalf of the group and ourselves, and I hope we passed the audition." Considering who they were and the significance of the moment I found this ironic, humorous, and, most of all, a rather humble statement.

Paul: (Paul personalized the event when he stoically responded to my seatmate for the event and his bandmate's wife Maureen Starkey's cheer.) "Thanks Mo."

John: (He was obviously being both relaxed and real because he knew every word, look, note, and comment was being taped and recorded. Maybe there was a bit of defiance against the norm, but he reveals his discomfort from the cold with these two comments.) "Oh, my soul, so hard," (after a rocking performance of "I've Got a Feeling") and "Thank you, brothers…hands too cold to play the chords" (after "Dig a Pony").

John was the most verbal during the brief time on the roof, probably because he was the one who was most emotionally disturbed by the whole situation, and, as is typical at times, the most unrestrained when vocalizing his feelings. I say this because John later said that he thought the whole Get Back/*Let It Be* project had to be "the most miserable sessions on Earth."

I was witnessing all this from a few feet away and I was mesmerized.

Now, per my invitation, Brent Stoker takes us back to that moment and, once again, I am captivated by its lingering melody.

Take it Brent…

Ladies and gentlemen…The Beatles!

TAKING IT TO THE ROOF

(BRENT STOKER)

Music fans in general and Beatles fans in particular treasure the rooftop concert. The only live, not-in-studio (recording, film, or television) performance the band gave during their last three years of existence is a brilliant snapshot of who they were all along.

And who were they? They were four extraordinary musicians who instinctively knew how to draw out the best of each other.

In spite of the acrimony and (according to John Lennon) pure creative boredom evident on screen throughout the film *Let It Be*, and musically in some of the numerous subsequently released recordings, there is a real creative spark in evidence on the rooftop. Maybe we shouldn't be at all surprised that, when push came to shove, they pulled it off in spectacular fashion. As George Harrison said about the four of them in the *Beatles Anthology*, "We were tight. That was one thing to be said about us. We were really tight, you know, as friends. We could argue a lot amongst ourselves, but we were very, very close to each other."

It helps too that the sound quality is so good. Given the laissez-faire attitude the Fabs demonstrated throughout a great deal of the *Let It Be* project, in addition to the technical glitches that plagued the project, one might expect poor sound quality and/or subpar performances. But the whole thing sounds great (as was the *Let It Be...Naked* album released decades later). The vocals are prominent and clear, mics for all three guitars were positioned well, Billy Preston's electric piano fits extraordinarily well in the mix, and Ringo's drums skins are expertly tuned and sound rich and full.

The film crew's Nagra professional audio recorders were, of course, also capturing all the music and ambient sound that day, but recording engineers Alan Parsons and Glyn Johns really get credit for capturing the music in such pristine quality audio that breezy Thursday in what was not the best of conditions. Alan fed the mass of cables carrying the sound to the basement Apple studio control room, where long-time Beatles producer George Martin and Glyn Johns were quietly tucked away, ensuring that two eight-track tape machines preserved whatever the band played.

As musicians, the Beatles were classy and empathetic players. They had a strong command of this day's material (John's lyric-lapses notwithstanding) and their playing is spot-on.

Performances of "Get Back" and "Don't Let Me Down," which became the A and B sides of the next Beatles single, to be released a few months later, dominate the rooftop proceedings. Those two songs accounted for five of the nine takes that day. Three of "Get Back" were performed, though one was only to check sound levels and balance, while "Don't Let Me Down" received two passes. They had recorded the official Apple single versions with Billy Preston's signature keyboard on these songs a few days prior, and no doubt knew they would be able to use some of the day's footage for promotional films, synching these live performances to the official tracks. This proved to be the case.

George's "For You Blue" is his song from this period that would have fit perfectly in the set list that chilly day, and what a treat that would have been. Maybe he didn't have the spirit to fight for the mic and take control away from the dominant frontline of Lennon and McCartney. It's also possible he figured a Harrison-fronted number would be edited from the final product; so why bother? Inclusion of the song must have been considered at some point; John's Hofer Hawaiian lap guitar, played during "For You Blue" earlier in the film, is visible in rooftop concert photos resting on a chair, waiting to be called in to action.

The inclusion of "One After 909" throughout *Let It Be* indicates they figured they probably didn't have enough up-to-par material, due to the fact that the massive thirty-song *"White Album"* recorded barely three months earlier had wiped them clean. They needed something new and pulled "909" out of their unreleased past. It's one they recorded properly, but unsatisfactorily, in 1963. Unhappy with that recording, they tucked it away for nearly six musically adventurous years. The song was no doubt resurrected because it fit the stated ethos of *Let It Be*: something that could be recorded without overdubs or studio trickery. This version's slight rhythmic swing gives it the needed kick in the pants that the 1963 version didn't have, and Billy Preston's electric piano weaves in and out of John and Paul's playful vocals. George really shines on "909" as well. No doubt his sharp guitar licks and flourishes on this performance far surpass anything else he did throughout the rest of the *Let It Be* project. But the entire band cooks on this one. It was mighty cold up there, and they did it in one take! Remarkable!

"Dig a Pony" gives us the Lennon-esque lyrics the writer excelled at, just the kind of word-play he would deride years later. "It was literally a nonsense song," he said to writer David Sheff in 1980, dismissing it as "another piece of garbage." Of course, most Beatles' fans love it and the nonsense therein. One man's garbage…

We get our last live taste of Beatles three-part harmonies in "Don't Let Me Down." On this track, we hear the only George Harrison rooftop vocals; and George's descending guitar work throughout the verses is particularly striking.

"I've Got a Feeling" is the true Lennon-McCartney collaboration played on this day. Specifically, Paul had a song (the "I've got a feeling" and bridge part) and John had a song (the "Everybody had a hard year" part). The last verse features a melodic interaction the Beatles were often so good at: counterpoint, wherein the different melodies performed at the same time have musical lines with strongly independent identities. As always, John and Paul's voices are gold against each other.

Their iconic instruments are in place—John's Epiphone Casino, which fans first saw during the 1966 world tour; Paul's '63 Hofner bass, for this period featuring on its face a BASSMAN sticker Paul borrowed from a Fender Bassman amplifier; George's beautiful Fender Telecaster, a special rosewood model the manufacturer had made especially for him; and Ringo's drums, a Ludwig five-piece maple finish Hollywood kit which were new as of this Beatles project. The bass drum was stuffed with a plaid blanket to muffle the sound. And it was the only time in a public Beatles performance (save for their formative years) when there was no drum skin with some logo, artwork, or color covering Ringo's bass drum.

Billy Preston's spirited playing on a Fender Rhodes suitcase piano adds so much light and life to the proceedings. As we know, Billy went on to a substantial solo career and was a featured player with assorted recordings and tours for decades to come, but these recordings, especially the studio versions of "Get Back" with "Don't Let Me Down" as the B-side, were surely his defining musical moment.

Of note, there's also a backup keyboard on the roof that gets no use. To George's side sits a Hohner Pianet N—a keyboard type used by the band as early as 1965 and most recently on their recording of John's "I Am the Walrus" more than a year earlier.

Ringo proves throughout why his drumming was perfect for this band and these songs—solid tempo throughout, and he plays nothing unnecessary; every drum fill and flourish is crisp and precise.

The set list is an interesting mix of composer credits. Although *Let It Be* is sometimes called a McCartney vanity project (John later said "That film was set up by Paul for Paul"), only the rooftop's "Get Back" and the first section of "I've Got a Feeling" are Paul's. Even though he was in a self-imposed creative funk, John still gets the dominant share of songwriting credit here: "Don't Let Me Down," the second section of "I've Got a Feeling," much of "One After 909," and most, if not all, of "Dig a Pony."

We'll never know how close we came to never having these performances. An unkind word or maybe an imposing logistical or technical issue could have kept the band quiet that day. It was winter in Central London after all; someone could have arrived that day with a terrible head cold. Filming might have ended in a huff with them never having shot the scene, thus leaving the project with no clear ending. The film and its recordings could have been shelved, incomplete for good. Brian Wilson's mid-1960s *Smile* project for the Beach Boys languished unreleased for decades. The *Rolling Stones Rock 'n' Roll Circus* film, also shot by director Michael Lindsay-Hogg only weeks prior to this Fabs' project, also sat for decades on the shelf because the Stones felt their own performance used to close the show was flat at best. It's conceivable *Let It Be* could have suffered the same fate.

But they did it. Overcoming internal strife and disillusionment, they climbed the stairs and gave solid performances of some great songs. Nine takes of five numbers. Three of the rooftop performances made the record virtually unaltered when it finally arrived more than a year later: "I've Got a Feeling," "One After 909" and "Dig a Pony," two of them ("909" and "Pony") performed that day in only one take each.

The entire sequence, legendary to fans forever as the "Rooftop Concert," is identified in photographs of the event handwritten on the crew's traditional wooden slate clapperboards simply as "Apple Films LTD—Beatles Show."

Much has been made of John Lennon's flippant yet brilliant parting remarks that day: "I'd like to say, 'thank you' on behalf of the group and ourselves. I hope we've passed the audition." Paul McCartney once made the observation that something in their story was "very John." Certainly, this line, too, was "very John."

It's not surprising that the man who started it all brought the story full-circle, uttering the last words we were to hear on the last released Beatles recording. Was the whole Beatles experience just an "audition" for us all?

Or, maybe it was, as John wrote and sang in 1966, "…the end…of the beginning."

STREET SCENE

Moving away from the small epicenter of activity on top of 3 Savile Row, people stood on adjoining rooftops, ledges, fire escapes, and at windows of nearby buildings. I noticed at first the stunned and confused looks on the faces of the people from the very adjacent building tops. This was immediately followed by astonished realization of what they were witnessing. Then, as others joined them, the early ones would turn to fill in the newcomers that the Beatles were playing live on their rooftop.

The most bewildered partakers were on the street directly below. They could only see glimpses of the film crew at the edge of the roof but they could hear what was going on…and it was loud and "blasting," as more than one observer reported. Without the aid of a visual, their initial response was simply a confused, "What the heck's going on?"

Next were the non-interested and immensely perturbed business people along the banker and tailor-laden Row that just wanted the bloody noise to stop. The predictable reaction was for a couple of them to call the Bobbies stationed at the West End Central Police Station located down the street, and insist they shut the bloody thing down! It's interesting that although the Bobbies were expeditiously dispersed to 3 Savile Row per their request, there was a sizable time lag between the time they "stormed" the building and when the music was finally shut down. The merchants probably figured the delay was due to a determined resistance from the Apple crew and heated discussions concerning legalities, sound laws, nuisance ordinances, and the like, but the truth is the Bobbies were having fun and loved being there, and were very cooperative in "letting 'er rip" and riff for a while. Mal could charm the fins off a fish, and you can see in pictures he and the English Bobbie, who was the first responder, leisurely standing by and coordinating the right moment to call it to a close. Afterward, when it did eventually become "unplugged," I can just picture the stiff-necked suits down below marching away with great pride thinking that they shut it down. After all, their fancy words had been forcefully said and their dirty deed was done, so the rigid upper crust "mob" naturally thought that they ruled the day's outcome, when, in actuality, they were out maneuvered by a laid back "bob" who had them fooled. The prime suspects of this backward victory were a highly influential and connected nearby bank executive along with Apple's next-door neighbor (1 Savile Row) Gieves & Hawkes, pre-eminent English tailors, 200 years standing.

As I've mentioned before, when I found out I was going up to the roof, I ran out the door dressed in a loaner coat and my basic California duds to the nearest clothing store I could find to buy a topcoat. I have zero recollection about the shop I came to first, or how far away it was from 3 Savile Row, because I was in a hurry, so it could possibly have been Gieves & Hawkes next door. I do remember the transaction was brief and curt. Because the merchants knew I was from Apple and a visiting American (I naively surmised I would get privileged treatment, maybe even a discount by disclosing this information) they sold me a white raincoat whose main purpose was simply to protect one from the rain and had nothing to do with body warmth, which makes me wonder if they got a kick out of doing the Yankee tourist in. I hope for irony's sake these particular merchants were indeed the tattletales next door, so that, in some obscure way, Mal got even for me in the end by his extended efforts above being so troubling to them.

One of our associates, who was unaware the concert had been planned, was coming to the office to work, and I remember him saying that as he rounded the corner from Vigo Street onto Savile Row he was "hit with a wall of sound."

Activity, movement, and purpose were altered, embraced, or ignored by those down below. Unless you were a fan and figured it out quickly, the whole affair was a mixture of mystery and confusion. Life as it was previously known on that block was brought to a complete halt by the screeching guitars wailing into the sky over everyone's heads. Some of the hipper "street people" were enthralled upon the realization of what was happening and, in spite of the frigid temperature, stopped in their tracks with eyes looking up, trying to get a glimpse or visualize the scene above them. They figuratively became frozen in place within the space of the moment. Also ignoring dampness and bitter winter chill were those who threw windows (of cars and buildings) open, along with all caution, to enjoy their "window seats," while others came out on the ledges or jumped out of their cars for a moment so they could hear better. People above and traffic below joined the abnormality by simply stopping what they were doing or were driving. It was surrealistic in a cold and clammy way.

Now, to be honest, and even a little sympathetic, it wasn't all "Ob-La-Di, Ob-La-Da, life goes on" on the street below. It was definitely a diverse gathering, a mixture of the enthralled who loved it and the enraged who wanted the unwelcome event to be shut down...now! I couldn't see them or hear their comments, but I can just visualize some very uptight scrunched up faces with hard-edged utterances spewing forth about propriety, decency, and the acceptable proper order in the way things were to take place on Savile Row. Those in charge of law and order were called upon to keep the peace, and, in addition to the clamor, the mounting traffic congestion was becoming a safety issue. As in all matters unstoppable, life goes on and things up high and things down low are not always in tune...but, the band rocked on, above it all in more ways than one.

Although there appeared to be a lot of confusion surrounding the event, I noticed a point of calm within the storm. Ringo had a limited view from his cold and windy backline perch, but he could see that the people watching from the adjacent buildings were really enjoying it, and that was good enough for him. Because he appeared to me to be both detached and into it that day, I sensed that his state of mind allowed him to have his own simplistic perspective. His arms and hands instinctively knew exactly what they were supposed to do, so his eyes and mind were free to scan the landscape as an observer...and he liked what he saw.

There is no denial that the timing of our local "roof-rock fest" was clearly designed to take place during the lunchtime in order to have the maximum crowd on the streets below, and that definitely magnified things a bit. Apple wanted to accomplish more than creating a film; in typical Beatles fashion, they wanted to create a commotion, stop traffic, cause a stir, and…complete a mission.

And, as John Lennon would say, make sure "everybody had a good time."

MISSING IN ACTION

To give an example of how casual this whole affair was, and in some ways a prime indication of how chaotic communication within the organization was at that time, some of the Apple staffers worked straight on through the whole happening without realizing, or just ignoring, what was happening above them, seemingly oblivious to the commotion taking place on the stairways and the roof. Others were aware and involved, even had something to do with putting it together, but for whatever reason missed the main event. That's like setting up the fireworks display but missing the fireworks. In other words, they weren't "up there" when the event "went down."

What appeared to me as being an astonishing lack of import attached to the rooftop event was Derek Taylor's posture that day. To some he appeared very detached from the whole affair, which was a press officer's dream. In retrospect, I believe Derek Taylor was a consummate pro at his crafty craft, and I also believe he knew exactly what he was doing. Considering the fact that there was no extra room on the roof and the press might have interrupted filming with crowd commotion and flashbulbs popping, or, worse yet, with the noise and clamor of bodies crashing to the floor below from the added body weight, Derek simply might have decided to keep a lid on the day's activities until a more strategic time. Also, something that only a press guy might consider is the uncomfortable fact that if he had put the word out, knowing the obviously massive turn out that would have ensued, he could have caused mammoth bad relations by turning down access to some of the people he needed on board to publicize the event when it was over. I'm sure he knew he had to be in his office to man the phones when rumor got around that the Beatles were making a ruckus at 3 Savile Row, and his many publicity contacts would be calling to find out what was going on.

Derek's third floor office was essentially the nerve center of the building, and he was used to holding court in his big wicker chair, as the excitement center of activities more than often emanated out of that area. Derek was typically in front of, on top of, or behind all things big in Apple and Beatles happenings, and it just doesn't make sense that he would choose to sit there while one of their biggest moments was going on two floors above. He was the constant, expected, and recognizable face on most things Beatles and Apple. To me, Derek Taylor had more real magic going on in his little finger than "Magic" Alex ever mustered up with his whole mind, body, and intentions.

It was not difficult to notice another major player in the day's happenings who was not up there—legendary Beatle producer George Martin. He was actually hunkered down in the basement recording studio at the building's furthest point away trying to make a record. I know he was very concerned about possibly getting escorted to the nearby police station and being locked up for disturbing the peace. That's why he felt more comfortable being at arm's (and leg's) length from the goings on upstairs and thereby didn't venture north to take a peek. It was quintessential George Martin—taking a gentlemanly subdued approach to a chaotic situation. He knew that the police were stationed a few doors away and figured it would only be a matter of time before they joined the fray. So, he laid low in the building by planting himself in that bottommost spot with Glyn Johns, as far away from the scene of the crime as possible. Strategically, I imagine he had calculated that the police could make it up the stairs to the roof quicker than he could escape down the same stairs to the street exit. He expressed a certain amount of distaste for the idea of spending his valuable time at the Savile Row police station. It's been reported that his face turned "a whiter shade of pale" when he heard that the police had entered the building.

As we tally up the important missing mainstays, in a personal sense Neil Aspinall's absence was the most surprising to me at the time, especially since I thought (maybe mistakenly) he was involved in getting equipment up to the roof earlier. But he did have a very valid excuse: he was having his tonsils taken out in a local hospital. It was still unusual though because typically Neil was everywhere all the time when it came to his long-time mates' activities. In some way I always felt Neil, like Mal, was unceasingly a few feet away, physically, emotionally, mentally, or even intuitively, when it came to "the lads." My best conclusion (because I have heard so many interpretations of his timeline in this matter) is that it was a pure emergency or he would have been there and his presence as always would be felt.

As I write this fifty years later, sadly these old dear friends have passed on. I can only surmise what their take on it would be now. How wonderful it would be if I could sit down today with each one of them and reminisce about those days.

I recently asked Peter Asher where he was that day because I have no memory of seeing him around the building. He told me he was in LA for an extended time in January 1969. (I did take note that his long business trip from London was to sunny southern California in the heart of winter.) He said that between various appointments and activities he would use my office on Hollywood and Vine while I was working out of a vacant office at 3 Savile Row.

These comings and goings were natural to quite a few of us, at a time when bouncing back and forth between London and LA was not that common. I love how so many of us have trouble recalling specific details about what might be considered major moments, but it's all because there was so much going on at the time. The nice thing about writing this book is that, because I am not a reporter or researcher, my primary goal is to share my reflections on a little piece of history I got to experience, and my secondary driving motive has been to get back in touch with old friends to see how we remember these things we haven't discussed in decades.

In my chat with Peter I mentioned that I was curious why Derek took such a laid-back approach. Peter said he didn't give it much thought. Even though he was on another continent at the time, his impression matches other comments in that he said he thought the event was more of a last-minute thing than most people realize.

Tony Bramwell, head of films and promotion, said he decided to distance himself from the ruckus and sit it out in his office, alternately watching the scene unfold from his window or going outside to the street below. When I asked Tony about his whereabouts during the concert he said, "When the concert began, I went out to the street to watch the public's reaction to the music. I went inside and took some calls from the BBC who wanted to know what was going on and invited them to come over and see. Then the police came in and stopped everything so we had a little media party in my office, and that was about it."

Barbara O'Donnell (Barbara Bennett at the time) spent her days in one of the main nerve centers of the Apple building. She was Peter Brown and Neil Aspinall's secretary (and consequentially had similar responsibilities with the four Beatles), and today would be known as the executive assistant to two of Apple's top executives and board members. She was a Liverpool neighbor from nearby Widnes and moved to London when she was seventeen. Barbara responded to an ad in the New Musical Express and landed a job on April Fool's Day serving as Brian Epstein's secretary until his death.

"On my first day at NEMS, Tony Bramwell had returned from holiday and he complained as they had given me his desk. That is all how it started," Barbara said recently.

It is almost impossible to imagine what she experienced over the years being part of the heart and soul of the Beatles phenomenon.

She described her activities on the day to me like this: "The day the boys played on the roof, my friend Laurie, a fellow Apple employee and long-time friend from NEMS, and I had gone to lunch in Soho. We used to frequent a little cafe there that was cheap and cheerful and full of prostitutes and lesser mobsters—we knew them all, always had a good laugh. On our return to Savile Row the street was full of people looking up and the Beatles were already playing. I asked Peter Brown if I could go and take a look as he was just about to pop up there. His answer was 'No,' because I was needed in reception to talk to the police that had just arrived. I was supposed to delay and placate them, so I never did see them perform."

I have listed below various possible reasons why some Apple staffers were not on the roof for the concert and it looks like Barbara fits in three or four of those categories.

As an interesting side note, Barbara told me that she had been up there quite a few times before, once when John changed his name from Winston to Ono—she was the witness! So, Barbara O'Donnell has her own roof story because she was one of the very few who were up there on another historical day.

Maureen Starkey and Yoko Ono did join us on the roof. I expected to see Yoko there but was a little surprised to see Maureen, especially without Pattie Harrison and Linda Eastman on site. Knowing those two, there may have been a sale at Harrod's and they went off shopping.

As previously stated, I have come up with a selection of explanations, both concrete and conjecture for why some Apple staffers didn't go up on the roof for the concert. Rather than try to pontificate any further on the myriad of reasons why some were absent that day, here is my list so that learned Beatles aficionados and knowers of all things Fab Four can assign numbers to their favorite MIAs.

1. Most employees weren't allowed for reasons of space, weight, and confusion.

2. Some didn't know it was happening.

3. Many had no idea how historic or monumental the event was going to be.

4. It was too cold. Who wanted to go up on a dirty, cold, rooftop five stories up on a stormy miserable day?

5. A few were so used to exciting things happening in the building that…ho, hum, just another Beatles thing.

6. They weren't invited!

7. Unfortunately, they picked the wrong time to be out for lunch.

8. Had other appointments or obligations.

9. Actually didn't care (Permutation of No. 5).

10. Really didn't want to. (Resultant conjectural permutation of No. 5 and No. 9 blended into No. 10).

11. Considered their job as being real employment, so were busy doing what they were supposed to be doing. (Total speculation on my part. Highly unlikely.)

12. Stoned or drunk and they missed it.

(My unofficial survey revealed that No. 1 and No. 12 sufficiently covered most of the staffers!)

NOT MISSING THE ACTION

So, a few big apples didn't make it to the market that day, but Michael Lindsay-Hogg's film footage and Ethan Russell's still photography, plus memory and researchers' detailed analysis, essentially validate the people who were actually there with the band in the immediate area created for the Beatles and the main event, excluding police (Ken Wharfe, Ray Shayler, and Peter Craddock, as far as I know) plus other possible workers from the film and sound crew. (I do apologize to anyone that may have been overlooked or that could not be identified. We did our best.)

- Alan Parsons – Sound engineer

- Anita Kass – Mrs. Ron Kass

- Billy Preston – Guest artist

- Chris O'Dell – Audience member (Staff)

- Dave Harries – Technical engineer

- Ethan Russell – Photographer

- George Harrison – Beatle

- Jack Oliver – Apple Executive

- John Lennon – Beatle

- Keith Slaughter – technical engineer

- Ken Mansfield – Audience member (Apple US)

- Kevin Harrington – Beatles equipment manager

- Mal Evans – Apple Executive

- Maureen Starkey – Audience member (Ringo)

- Michael Lindsay-Hogg – Film Director

- Paul McCartney – Beatle

- Peter Brown – Apple Executive

- Ringo Starr – Beatle

- Ron Kass – Apple Executive

- Tony Richmond – Director of Photography

- Yoko Ono – Audience member (John)

It was a once-in-a-lifetime occurrence that will live on, not only in our memories, but also deep in our hearts.

Talk about a day in our lives!

BRICKS AND MORTALS

ROUGH MIX

To my mind Alan Parsons was the ultimate producer, engineer, and master craftsman when it came to contemporary recorded sound. In my early years as a record producer I was fascinated by his techniques, especially when it came to echoes and digital delays. When I hear one of his recordings I immediately recognize who I am listening to, or perhaps I should say, whose sound creation I am experiencing.

When Alan has his hands on a recording, you can sonically hear and feel his touch. Take, for example, his groundbreaking work on Pink Floyd's legendary *Dark Side of the Moon*. The everyday listener may not have noticed Alan's panning techniques or creative equalization prowess on that record, but they definitely heard something so special in the incredible combination of production, performance, and engineering that, to this day, the album continues to hold the record, by far, for the most charted weeks on the *Billboard 200*: 917 weeks. Now think about it; that's a little more than seventeen and a half years! No other album has even come close to touching that record…not even the Beatles.

Here's the way Alan described it in our interview: "The success of a record is a team effort. It's not the sound but the songs and the performance of that band at that moment in time. I do what I always do and act on instincts and that's just how it came out." It's not often I would disagree with Alan Parsons in production matters, and in this case, it is only his humility I question, not his creative contribution. The sound *on Dark Side of the Moon* is the first thing that jumped out at me, and then on subsequent listenings (thousands perhaps?), the magnitude of the total performance and craftsmanship became more apparent. But that's just me. There is no one way to describe the impact this offering had on Rock 'n' Roll…a new standard had been set.

If I were a boxer, I could only aspire to be as good as Muhammad Ali, knowing I could never be as good as the champ. That was how I felt when it came to Alan Parsons. I am not talking about production competition, but dedicated aspiration to achieve greatness in a fascinating craft. Here's what's interesting: when discussing production techniques with artists, engineers, and other produces, I would mention my admiration for Alan's recording prowess and his body of work. Invariably, I would be asked if we were friends or if I had met him. The assumption was a natural one because of our mutual involvement with Apple and other British artists. It always surprised them when I answered no and, in fact, I was also surprised because of being in the same studios and entertainment circles that we both ran in for so many years.

But, as wonderful happenstance would have it, we did finally meet, and the meeting turned out to be more interesting than I had expected. Fortunately for my sanity, the entertainment business and I got tired of each other at the same time, and in the process, I almost seamlessly morphed out of producing records to becoming an author and speaker. But one day, almost thirty years from my rooftop experience, I received an email from John Montagna, who was Alan's bass player for his touring Alan Parson's Project at that time. John was a fan of one of my books in which I had mentioned, somewhat as I am doing now, how I looked up to Alan's expertise in the studio. Because of this comment he said he would send me the band's itinerary, and if we were ever in proximity while touring on the road, to let him know and I would be his guest.

Well, it wasn't long before we were less than 100 miles apart and I took him up on his offer. I loved the show (great seating, as being the artist's guest is always a nice touch) and was definitely looking forward to meeting my sonic hero. Even though my producing days were over, I was still a fan. I anticipated a brief hello, mixed with a summary of obvious mutual friends and studios, and then I would be on my way. One obvious mutual experience was time spent with the Beatles, and during our conversation we discovered that we were on the roof together.

We were both quite surprised when we found out that we were veterans of a very special engagement and developed a unique camaraderie because of that shared experience. The roof event took place before my transition from music biz executive to entering into a full-time production career. At that time Alan was still in the process of "making his bones" as an engineer and producer and was pulling cables and setting mics that day for Glyn Johns and George Martin. I paid him little attention, and he couldn't have cared less about who the "suits" were on the roof. We said nary a hello nor exchanged a head nod that day and went on our ways until this moment of our get-together thirty years later.

We agreed on one thing for sure in our meeting: Alan said he also believed, like me, that hooking up with the Beatles was an extremely fortunate case of timing.

"I just happened to apply at the studios at the right time, and I think I had the right credentials in what they were looking for," said Alan, who was nineteen at the time he applied, "I had a bit of experience with the tape machine. Working with the Beatles was a lucky, fortunate break for me."

I can't tell you how many times I have heard this type of story surrounding the way individuals ended up working for the Beatles. People would be brought into their thunderous world based on the most casual meeting or circumstance, or an interview type of situation, where very little substantiated experience was offered by the interviewee.

Alan was willing to pay his dues and the system at Abbey Road Studios, where he was learning his craft, made sure of it. No one moved up the ladder quickly at the EMI-owned facility, but it was a system that ended up paying dividends for all the personnel who hung in there. Many later became famous engineers and producers.

"It was more about the people than the place, because the training you received at Abbey Road was second to none," he said. "Just about everybody who trained there became somebody and had success in the music business. It just has a certain magic and it's still there to this day."

When the Beatles moved to 3 Savile Row, they wanted to transfer Abbey Road's magic to the basement of the building by creating a studio. They got a different kind of magic instead: "Magic Alex" Mardas.

I was introduced to Alex, a Greek exile who headed up the Apple Corps' consumer electronics division during one of my earliest visits to Apple. I met him over a meal with Ron Kass at Tiddy Dols Eating House in the nearby Shepherd's Market area of Mayfair. Two firsts took place for me that day—eating Welsh Rarebit and watching someone write formulas and graphics on the restaurant's white tablecloth with his blue pen while simultaneously enjoying Tiddy Dol's famous hot spiced gingerbread. Picture a mad scientist with a sweet tooth having a sugar rush while experiencing an equational epiphany.

It's strictly my opinion, but Alex wrote many checks with his words that his hands could not possibly cash. He had startling creative ideas that definitely proved ahead of their time. He spoke about inventing a phone that dialed by voice recognition and displayed the phone numbers of callers; an artificial sun using laser beams; a memory phone with an electronic camera; a flying saucer with invisible coating; wallpaper speakers; electrical paint; a musical toilet, and on and on and on. He was always working on something, finishing nothing—promising a lot, producing little. The reality of the situation was that he could never deliver. Perhaps the real problem lay in the fact that he had no electronics background (though he was highly educated). One of his other enticements was that he was going to build a futuristic, state-of-the-art, 72-track studio in the basement of Apple, which was unheard of back then. (Abbey Road and most other studios were still eight-track at the time).

Alex, in the amusing non-reality of those days, was the ultimate con man of sorts. That may be a harsh term to describe him, and it didn't come from me, but he fascinated everyone with all these incredible things he was going to invent or put together. Nothing ever worked or materialized that I am aware of. The first invention I remember hearing about was Ringo's new phone that was supposedly in the works when I first got to Apple. The way the gadget was described to me at that time was a simpler version from what I mentioned above, but he said he had developed a phone where Ringo could just talk to it and it would dial the person he wanted to talk to. Now even this in itself was real spacey stuff in those days!

The most dramatic item, and the one that excited me the most, was a creation that not only the Beatles would benefit from but something that the record business needed badly, as the era of making bogus copies of albums and reselling them at a cheaper price was upon us. This invention would bring record pirating to a screeching halt. Alex explained, over lunch and between scribbles, that he had developed a method where all Apple albums recorded would include the music and a separate spoken message that would be simultaneously embedded into their records, along with the album content, when they were pressed. A corresponding signal would be added to this secondary information that would cancel it out, so it would be masked, and that way the owner of the legitimate product wouldn't hear the two signals of added information, just the music…but, if someone tried to copy the record, the canceling signal would not record during the transfer, making the intended recorded music ruined by two pieces of information playing at once. It was even said that Alex could have the unwanted portion say things like, "Oh, so you are trying to steal our music, eh? Well, we caught you and want you to know the Beatles think you are a creep and a cheapskate! Now go and buy the record you low level loser!" But he did bring these exciting magical expectations into the building and was soon knighted as "Magic Alex" by John Lennon, the most cynical of the four lads.

So, having lunch at a restaurant that day did end with the tablecloth being covered with formulas and scrawls, and at that point I thought it was an indication of his genius. They probably had no real meaning, just more of his baloney. But, when you add Alex's antics into the mix of movie stars, Hell's Angels, the occasional nude teenager running about, talented artists, Hare Krishnas, losers, and other loonies wandering the halls of offices of the building, I found myself in a pretty amusing environment. At Apple, all things appeared possible and, in some cases, even normal. There was also a smell wafting about that, after breathing its sweet essence for a while, you couldn't help but just be happy you were there.

Well, like most of his promised "magical" endeavors, Alex's 72-track studio for the Beatles never panned out. The mixing console, though it looked cool, didn't work, the room was not soundproofed, and the heating system that sat in the corner continued to thump loudly. The Beatles were literally in a jam. George Martin made a call to Abbey Road and requested the proper recording equipment be sent over ASAP.

Alan recalled technical engineers hoisting two old consoles into the studio, hooking up a mobile recording unit from Abbey Road, which wasn't booked that week. Another eight-track deck was procured, and they were joined together to bring the Beatles sixteen tracks.

Whenever new Beatles recordings would land on my desk at Capitol Hollywood, I was always amazed at the incredibly innovative sound that would pour forth from my speakers. When I saw the equipment they worked with, especially at Abbey Road, I was even more amazed by the technical limitations the Beatles worked with, in so many instances, and the incredible product that was produced by them during their time.

The conversation with Alan naturally switched to the *Let It Be* sessions, which Alan remembers wasn't entirely miserable. He says they were a fun group of people, a band of merry pranksters who were always ready to pull a gag or two. This lighthearted thing was always waiting in the wings with the Beatles.

Alan said he had very little time to prepare for the rooftop concert, and worked late into the night to make it happen in his capacity as second engineer on *Let It Be*. Part of his job was to run multiple cables from the basement up to the roof, and after they were properly in place, I was privileged to occupy an historic and very special space with him on that extraordinary day. Upon our discovery of this proximal fact, the dynamics of our conversation changed. Being on the roof together made us like two guys who shared a foxhole in World War II. We experienced a life-changing event that created a lasting special bond. What is cool about that now is that, fifty years later, we are among the few who are still here to talk about it.

One other item that especially pleases me has to do with his recollections of what it was like working with the Beatles and the people who surrounded them on a daily basis. Looking back, we share the same lasting impression: their lighthearted, easy-going, and upbeat nature.

Something else I believe Alan and I agree on is that it was not so much about what we saw when looking at the Beatles; it's what we experienced when they were looking at us. Another way to say that is when we were around them, they politely conveyed a feeling of inclusion that made us feel we were a part of their determinations and passion.

We got a feelin'…oh, yeah!

ROOFTOP REDHEAD

History can bring us to our knees or it can set us on high places. A single instance, incident, moment, day, or isolated event can change an ordinary person into someone of great interest and stature. Kevin Harrington, like the rest of us, happened into a great job; the money wasn't that good, but the thrills, camaraderie, and subsequent great memories made up for that.

Like so many of the people I met and worked with briefly at Apple, our everyday moves went roaring by like a blur. We were often caught up into important things together while at the same time barely bouncing off of or touching upon each other in the whirl of it all. A great example of this…he is "the redhead on the roof" standing next to me "the guy in the white coat."

To me, Kevin was a mini-version of Mal. Now, if I am comparing anyone to Mal Evans you obviously know by now that the comparison is of a positive nature. Kevin took care of lot of stuff that Mal used to handle in the beginning (we all start somewhere).

I was thirteen years older than Kevin, but there is something about the music business that keeps a person young inside. There is also another element that seems to minimize age differences that would normally create a communication chasm between a young man still in his teens and a foreigner in their early thirties. Kevin and I were in the same bubble of time sharing a common passion when watching our bosses at work. There was a technical difference though that had nothing to do with job titles, and I didn't find this out until he told me about it recently. In a recent chat, he corrected a comment I made in an interview years ago where I referred to him as an Apple staffer. I assumed he worked for Apple, but he was actually in the direct employ of the Beatles (hired personally by Mal Evans) and didn't have to concern himself with the Apple doings, or any politics or positioning that might be going on there.

Kevin was born during a very difficult time in post-war London in a council floor maisonnette (subsidized housing), and times were so austere that his mother was forced to cut the umbilical cord as she waited for a midwife to arrive. Naturally, growing up, he was scarred by the psychological remnants left behind on the British people, caused by the devastation the country experienced at the hands of the German Luftwaffe who led almost nightly bombings and air raids in 1940 and 1941. I'm sure his parents lived every day with the fear that death was just around the corner. Kevin's father died of tuberculosis when Kevin was two.

At the end of the war, parts of London were reduced to ruin and rubble. (Kevin spent many years playing on bomb sites in his youth.) It would be years before buildings were replaced with new construction, and decades before the country's economic situation was restored—the Beatles could take some credit for the country's financial improvement, which nicely binds Kevin to their story.

Leaving school to join the workforce at age fourteen, Kevin started off as an actor. He landed a part as an extra in a television show and worked on a BBC film on Hitler youth, but appendicitis stepped in and ended his acting career. (I guess you could say he started with "Mein Fuhrer" and later ended up with "Der Four.") He entered the music business a year later by answering an ad for an "Office Boy" in the Evening Standard. He phoned, put on his best suit and tie, and went in for an interview with Peter Brown, then office manager for NEMS, Brian Epstein's company. His first official day of work was January 24, 1966.

Kevin proved his worth almost immediately. He wasn't afraid to roll up his sleeves and do what needed to be done. He fetched mail, stuffed envelopes, posted letters, ran errands, and, every day before he got into work, picked up Peter Brown's mid-morning hot salt beef sandwich from a shop just off of Piccadilly Circus.

He worked his way up within NEMS from office boy to "Mr. Epstein's" personal assistant to stagehand at the Saville Theatre (which Brian Epstein, who studied acting, took over the lease in 1965) to being in put in charge of the Beatles' equipment from 1968 onward. He was described to me upon my arrival as the house roadie, jack of all things that needed to be done, and gofer extraordinaire. Going for needed items for Derek Taylor or John Lennon, for instance, was not a low-level job. This was Apple Records, London, the Beatles, and the eye of the Rock 'n' Roll hurricane during its most glorious years. He got paid by Apple for what about 90 percent of the young men of the day would gladly have paid Apple to do.

So, in the midst of passing by each other every once in a while, only one day stands out—the day he and I landed on top of an old building on Savile Row. For me it was the thrill of a lifetime, a special experience that I knew I was going to treasure for the rest of my life. For Kevin, it may not have been quite as romantic.

"It was just another day working for the Boys," is how Kevin succinctly put it. "I don't remember a set date for when we would be on the roof, but Mal did tell me there were plans to do a live show somewhere." Of course, that somewhere eventually turned out to be the roof, which presented a minor problem for Kevin who was in charge of lugging all the gear up to the top of a five-story building.

"On the day of filming it was relatively easy getting most of the gear up there, except for Billy's piano and Paul's bass cabinet," Kevin said. "The small staircase had a turn halfway up, and I couldn't get the bass cab or the piano over the right turn due to the banisters. That's when I called Mal for help."

After much heaving, it was decided that the only way up to the roof was straight through the skylight, though even that didn't work out, as it was a few inches too small, recalls Kevin. Mal then decided the window would have to be taken out. It turned out to be a good move.

"With a length of rope and a bit of heaving, we got them up," Kevin said.

So, there we were on the roof on a cold January day. I was huddled against the chimney with Chris, Yoko, and Maureen, as we held our breaths against the cold and the emotional aspect of the happening while Kevin can be seen holding up a sheet of lyrics for a forgetful boss. John Lennon needed his help so he could read the lyrics to "Dig a Pony," a new composition. On his knees with a damp, cold wind blowing through his curly red hair, dressed only in a sport coat and light-colored open-collar shirt, he stood tall among young men in a magic time of Rock 'n' Roll history. If that job sounds at all menial, then consider there probably wasn't one person within miles who would not have given their left ear or other functional body part just to take his place. If John Lennon had asked for volunteers to take on that particular task, I can just see Chris O'Dell and me jumping up from our seats, with hands raised yelling, "Pick me, pick me!"

There was a lot of nonchalance mixed in with the worldwide dynamics of the occasion going down that afternoon. To put that seemingly absurd word in perspective I will always lean on the one depiction I have repeated before about that day, and that is that it was "one of the most historical events in Rock 'n' Roll." So how could the word "nonchalance" have anything to do with describing anything to do with history in the making? Well…

We've already mentioned a number of involved Apple staffers who nonchalantly didn't bother to make it to the roof for the little hootenanny going on there. And you can also see the police officer standing casually by Mal Evans waiting for a time to come alive and "bust up" the noisy gathering. But the moment that nailed the word "nonchalance" to the extreme degree was when, to my subdued horror, I saw that picture (the cover of this book) of Kevin sitting on the wall having a ciggie while I was standing there beside him, having a little midday chat, barely three feet away from George Harrison…and I was not even looking at one of the most historical events in Rock 'n' Roll.

"And the award for the most inept, inappropriate, and unbelievable act of 'Sheer Nonchalance' goes to…Ken Mansfield!"

GET BACK GIRL

Peter Asher became an immediate friend the day I picked him and Gordon Waller up at LAX, when they came to California in 1965 as Capitol Records artists Peter and Gordon. Ironically, it was Peter Asher who picked me up at Heathrow Airport when I came to London in 1968 to work with Apple Records. It was my maiden voyage to Europe, so when I walked through that unfamiliar door at 3 Savile Row to work with a new company, because of him I didn't have the added burden of feeling like I was among strangers. At that point, I already had several friends in the building, and before long became lifelong friends with a few more.

I am country at heart—a true American westerner—and I have California written all over me. Historically, my family heritage is British Isles and any mixture of these environs is where I am most comfortable. I mention this because when I walked in to Peter Asher's fifth floor office at Apple I was introduced to his assistant, Chris O'Dell, who was all these things and beyond, and my comfort level immediately improved even more. As I later discovered, she was from Tucson, Arizona, but she sure looked like a California girl to me…blond, pretty, and sharp.

Chris O'Dell stood out from the flock of British "birds" that were flitting about the halls and offices of Apple. She had the class needed to work with someone like the gentlemanly Mr. Asher, the spark to keep the place lit up with her smile, and the smarts coupled with a hard work ethic that made you feel things within her sphere were getting done. She also had a natural congeniality so that when she was communicating with John, Paul, George, and Ringo, or anyone else at Apple, you could tell not only was she at ease, but they were too. I got the sense she was as welcome in their homes as she was in her own. In the midst of the extravaganza-like atmosphere of this amazing place I got the sense that there were two dependable worker bees on staff in the middle of a constant buzz: Chris O'Dell and Jack Oliver. I know there were others, but she and Jack were my personal company standouts. When we would all go out to the pubs later on at night I found these two were also standouts in that endeavor!

Chris and I laugh now about one exciting night when we went out partying at the posh, private club restaurant, Dell'Aretusa on Kings Road in Chelsea, but neither of us is sure who joined us. We know my late partner in crime from Hollywood, Larry Delaney, who was Derek Taylor's counterpart at Capitol Records, and Paul were part of the gang, but we had such a roaring time that night that we can't remember if they were the only ones or if any of the other Beatles were with us. It was like that then. Things were so over the top because the world we were living in at that time had such a numbing effect, to the point that our awareness wasn't the focus; it was Apple and its magic, and that became our separate reality. Do you remember who you went out with on August 17, 1968? At least Chris remembers the restaurant!

As I look back now, it's hard to believe that Chris and I have been friends for nearly a half-century. We were practically "babies"—she was a few years out of high school and I had just turned thirty. We both just happened to be in the right place at the right time, especially where Chris was concerned. Here's her backstory:

Chris was living in Hollywood at the time (I knew she was a California girl!), chilling on her sofa, watching a game show on her thirteen-inch black-and-white TV set, smoking a joint, and waiting for her boyfriend, Allan, to pick her up for a date. Allan was on the tardy side, two hours and counting, and despite the joint in her mouth, she wasn't exactly chill. She was very annoyed in fact.

When Allan finally phoned at 10:00 p.m., he was calling from the La Brea Inn; he was having drinks and smokes with a few friends and a British fellow named Derek Taylor. At the time, Derek was doing publicity for A&M Records and had worked for the Beatles a few years earlier. That last bit of information perked Chris's ears, but only for the fact she thought it was bogus information.

"The Beatles! Who knew anyone who worked for the Beatles?" Chris says today, with a smile in mock disgust.

Chris wasn't in the mood to venture out. She wanted a quiet evening alone with Allan, who was pleading with her to jump in the car and come meet them, especially Derek.

Chris spent a few moments staring at the lamp on the side table. Should she stay or should she go? She was really torn.

Smart girl that Chris was, she deduced anything would be better than sitting alone in her apartment on a Saturday night. So, she changed into her yellow-striped bell-bottom jeans and white top with puffy sleeves, touched up her makeup, jumped in her beige '68 Mustang, and headed for the Sunset Strip. It was a pivotal meeting that changed the trajectory of Chris's life.

Over drinks, Derek regaled everyone with his wild adventures with the Beatles, Paul Revere & The Raiders, Tiny Tim, the Doors, the Byrds, and Captain Beefheart. He also mentioned he was a few weeks away from leaving LA and heading back to London to work for the Beatles' new company, Apple Corps Limited.

When they closed down the La Brea Inn, the party moved to Derek's rented home in Laurel Canyon. It was there where Chris and Derek shared the eternal bond of smoking a joint together, a Hawaiian strand Derek called "Icebox," which Chris says was the strongest pot she'd ever had. That figures with Derek.

For the next three weeks, Chris was Derek's chauffeur by proxy (he didn't own a car and didn't know how to drive—a must in Los Angeles), tying up loose ends and running errands as he prepared to move back across the pond. Chris drove him to television and radio interviews, sat in on recording sessions, accompanied him to meetings with record producers and attorneys, and joined him for lunches, which often included celebrities. Chris was working at a record distributor and called in sick a few days to accompany Derek. After a while, she didn't even bother. She was having so much fun being with Derek, meeting so many new people and getting connected, she felt she could find a new job with no problem. (Oh, the confidence of the young!) And Chris was right. She eventually did find a new job…at Apple, based on Derek's hearty recommendation.

Getting to London was easier said than done. She had to convince her parents to support her decision and pay for her own airplane ticket, food, hotels, and taxis to get her through the first few weeks until she got situated. Adding to this anguish was the fact that Chris had no money in her savings and owned more money on her Mustang than it was worth. The only thing she had of value was her beloved record collection—music that gave her great joy and got her through some rough times.

It was a tough choice: adventures in England or the emotional comfort of a record collection? Chris knew what she had to do, so she sold the record collection to a friend of a friend for $200.

Her parents chipped in by selling her life insurance policy and agreed to take over her car payments. On May 17, 1968, two months after Derek Taylor left the City of Angels, Chris was chauffeured to the Tucson Airport by her parents and flew on a one-way ticket to London. It was a brave and crazy thing to do, but that pretty much sums up Chris.

On her first day at the 95 Wigmore Street office, she met Paul and John and Yoko—in that order. The closest Chris ever got to the Beatles was in the far reaches of the upper level of LA's Dodger Stadium, where she and her sister watched the Fab Four in concert on August 28, 1966. Even though the seats were in the nosebleed section, the noise was ear shattering.

"They came out of this van and you saw these little dots and you knew it was the Beatles," Chris says with a smile. "You really couldn't hear much and it was a short concert…but it was the fact that you were in the same space as the Beatles."

At Apple, she occupied the same space, but this time it was a much more intimate space, and instead of a one-night brief event, she was seeing a Beatle up close on almost a daily basis.

"Paul was the serious, heavy-duty Beatle and was at Apple every day, that was his thing," Chris said. "John was totally into Yoko and very involved with her and whatever projects they were doing. George was pretty much off into his spirituality, and Ringo was away doing a movie."

She recalls Apple as an exciting business enterprise that was the center of the universe in the late '60s—a place where you never knew what the next day would bring.

"The Beatles were so big that anyone would have wanted to be a part of it," Chris offers. "Almost everybody who worked there lived for that job, because it was such a great job to have. You never knew who was going to show up. You never knew which Beatle would show up. You didn't know what mood people were going to be in; what mood the Beatles would be in, or what they were going to ask you to do. So, it had that every day adventure feel to it."

And business came with a Rock 'n' Roll twist: a fully stocked bar, Cordon Blue chefs, bright green carpet, and Derek's wicker chair. She says before she was officially hired, she had to pass muster with an astrologer at the behest of John and Yoko.

"It was astrology, but I also remember Tarot cards," Chris recalls. "He wanted to know my birthday and other key dates. 'Where's your moon? Where's your Sun? Where's your Mercury?' Did it fit? Well, it fit."

Chris was a great fit, and along with Richard DiLello ("the house hippie"), and Ron Kass, they were the only Americans on full-time staff. She says that bode well for her because she worked at a much more competitive level than the English birds in the office, who were deferential and almost passive. Chris possessed a can-do spirit and "Let's get it done now" attitude, which set her apart.

"I was a little pushy. Back then, if you wanted something done as soon as possible, that took about two weeks…and that was to get something printed or copied," Chris says. "My thing was, 'No, we need it now.' So, I impressed others with my ability to get things done quickly." She was also impressive in the pubs and nightclubs, which is where I really got to know Chris.

Chris worked hard, played hard, and became very close with "the boys" and their loved ones, particularly George and Pattie Harrison. That closeness gave her a certain derring-do, like asking Paul McCartney if she could sit in on one of their recording sessions. A secretary who was nearby told Chris, "You can't do that. The recording sessions are closed. None of us are allowed to go into the studio." Chris was also rebuffed by Mal Evans, who greeted her at the studio when she showed up. This steely young lady not only entered the studio that night, but the Beatles asked her to add her handclaps to a track—"Revolution" on the "*White Album.*" A few months later, she joined the chorus on "Hey Jude."

When Chris first started at Apple, she was running errands, picking up people from the airport, collecting press clippings, and sometimes she relieved the switchboard operator; but then came her big break—she became Peter Asher's personal assistant and secretary. Peter was the head of Apple's A&R, and the man who discovered James Taylor. Chris's love for music and her previous job at a record distributor made her a natural for this position, so she started listening to tapes, recruiting groups, and booking studio time for the Beatles and other Apple artists. She was capable and super friendly...too friendly according to some.

"Peter's wife at the time was a lady named Betsy, an American from New York. She used to get mad at me because she thought I was too friendly to people on the phone," Chris explains. "Peter once said, 'Betsy thinks you're too friendly to people on the phone.' I said, 'I don't know how else to be.' Peter said, 'I don't have a problem with it,' and so it was dropped. Except when Betsy called, then I wasn't so friendly."

In time, Chris was accepted by all her peers, including the English birds who thought she might have been a little bit aggressive in the beginning. One of their first bonding experiences had to do with the Apple roof. Chris says that on warm summer days they'd venture to the roof of Apple, throw down a blanket, and work on their tans.

My eyes always light up at the mention of the roof because it conjures up all sorts of emotions for me. I've romanticized it, heralded it, and held it dear to my heart all these years. My reaction becomes even more emotionally charged when I am talking with an old friend, a lasting friend, a friend that I huddled close to and sat in awe with a cold five stories above the world as we experienced the ultimate musical event of the century together.

"It was filthy, dirty. It was, after all, a rooftop," Chris says. "It seems as if the ladder going up to the roof wasn't always there, and the stairs were little and scrawny. But it was really good if you wanted to go up there and sunbathe."

Chris remembers that the first time she heard of plans for a concert was at a meeting in the conference room at Apple. And it wasn't going to be the rooftop.

"There was a lot of talk about where they could go," she says. "The thing I remember most vividly is that they talked about doing the concert at the Grand Canyon. I was so excited because I thought, *Yes! the Beatles are gonna play the Grand Canyon in my home state.* I thought that was pretty cool. I remember it because, to me, that was home."

Well, we know how that one turned out. Chris guesses it was *Let It Be* director Michael Lindsay-Hogg or Director of Photography Tony Richmond who came up with the rooftop idea because they were the ones most actively scouting locations.

"The roof was the perfect choice," Chris says. "The Beatles could go anywhere else, and they wanted people to hear it…that was a very special place and a very special day."

Chris says she instinctively knew it would be an historic day, and did everything in her power to get up there on the roof, taking to cajoling, pestering, and dropping not-so-subtle hints to everyone who might have the juice to get her up there.

"I looked for events, and my mind was event-focused," Chris said. "I knew this was an important event in Beatle history…playing together live again after so long."

But Chris was not invited to the party and wasn't on the list. That tore it up for her as she watched many people traipse through her office with gear, amps, microphones, wooden planks, and hardware as they prepared for the filming. The dagger through the heart was a memo from Peter Brown essentially telling all staffers they were verboten from going up on the roof because of weight restrictions. That dictum was something that really stuck in Chris's craw and reduced her to tears.

"It was a gut-wrenching experience because here we are, working in the damn building and we can't go up to the roof and watch?" she said nearly fifty years later. "And all the excitement was happening on my floor."

Chris was given a lifeline by cameraman Tony Richard when he noticed her sitting at her desk, dabbing her eyes, looking dejected and defeated. Naturally, he asked what was wrong and why she was upset.

"We're not allowed on the roof," Chris said. "I can't go up there. Only essential staff are allowed."

"Well, I need an assistant," Tony smiled. "I'm giving you permission. Come with me."

"Are you serious?" she said. "Do you think it will be okay?"

Tony laughed, pulling her out of her seat. She grabbed her coat and followed Tony up the rickety steps.

When they reached the roof, Chris recalled Mal Evans was the only Apple staffer up there. Tony quickly set up his camera and told her to sit at an empty bench next to him. She was seated next to the building's chimney and a few feet away from the edge of the roof.

I was the next person to sit down on that bench. Chris remembered that I greeted her with a smile through my chattering teeth. She also recalls with great clarity my famous first words on the roof: "Damn, it's cold up here!"

Chris and I both recall that Paul was the first Beatle to appear, followed by Ringo and Maureen. John and Yoko were next, and then George and Billy Preston came up together. Within minutes the band began to play. For the first few minutes of the concert, Chris was still worried she was going to get yanked from the bench.

"I thought someone like Peter Brown was going to come up on the roof and say, 'You're not supposed to be here. Come back down.' I kept waiting for someone to kick me off, and then after a while I thought, No, I don't think they're going to."

Chris and I were situated barely a few feet from the Beatles and she sensed it wasn't long before the band knew this was history in the making.

"They were a band again," Chris said, "and even though it was so cold, they seemed to be enjoying themselves. It was a momentous occasion for the fact they knew it was going to be on film and forever."

Forever is the key word here, the ultimate essence and the final lingering impression. A famous jeweler's advertisement that has worked for years states: "Diamonds are forever." Well, so are golden moments and cold rooftops with wonderful people! Thanks Chris, I am glad we shared that bench.

OLIVER WITH A TWIST

I love the irony…while writing this book my friend Jack just flew in to Florida from LA so I could join him on his new film project. It's about the Beatles and Apple. I remember one time I flew in from LA to join him at Apple in London, and there was a film project going on there. It was about the Beatles and Apple. We also appeared together in a promotional film produced by my Nashville publisher ten years ago. It was about the Beatles and Apple. I moved from LA and live in Florida now. He moved from London and lives in LA and…it's fifty years later, and I am writing about…the Beatles and Apple.

Possibly my most lasting relationship after decades in the entertainment business is one from my very early years and comes from another continent. I find that fact a little odd, so I guess I'll just call it the Oliver twist.

Jack Oliver can be best described as a gentle, rascally man, or a rascally gentleman. He was, and still is, everything about being British and being a Londoner during its most raucous and vibrant times. Besides the enormous weight of our professional responsibilities, I now find that some of my favorite memories are about a time spent together in

London during the after-hours when we headed out the Apple door after a busy day to unwind at the hotspots that surrounded 3 Savile Row. We worked hard and partied even harder. I am not going to describe how we wound up after we got done winding down.

When I was managing Apple in LA he was keeping things on track at Apple in London. It was all business with us when it came to getting things done—that was the original bonding ground for our relationship. That bond remains today, intact like iron glue and here we are, going at it again, except we are moving a little slower and definitely more relaxed.

It's difficult not to get a little fluffy when I talk about old friends like Jack Oliver, Mal Evans, or Ron Kass, but some people get past a lot of our protective barriers, and what begins in many cases as business relations end up lodging deeper inside our being. Jack, to this day, still has that cynical English vibe, and he can be crusty at times, but I couldn't ask for a more loyal friend. Over the years when I would get ill, I'd receive a phone call or nice card from long-time friends and relatives. Jack, though, would always send flowers, and one time he sent a beautiful plant. I named the plant Jack and I kept it in my office. One day it died, and shortly afterward Jack called to say hello. I told him Jack died. He had forgotten about the plant and thought I meant our friendship was over! The point is that all of my close, long-time American friends gave me a nod when I was down, and crusty old Jack from another continent would send a thoughtful gift.

Out of everyone at Apple, Jack became my main guy when it came to getting things done as we worked across a great expanse—"the pond" as we called it—both of us trying to handle complicated logistics long distance in an orderly manner. The tasks tended to be a little difficult when attempting to organize chaos (i.e., getting four Beatles to agree on something). I think our combined dedication to the duties entrusted to us coupled with being able to set that aside and revel in the London nights together gave us a firm foundation for friendship. We've remained close, occasionally reliving those days in chats, hanging out, and reflections, but we have also watched and mourned the passing of so many friends that polished the Apple to its shining glory. Funnily enough, in all these passing years we never really discussed that day on the roof until now.

So that's a bit about how I saw, see, and came to know Jack. In our admittedly prideful recall, we have oft lamented how we felt overlooked in a lot of the historical reporting on Apple history, especially when done by information gatherers who weren't there, never even met a Beatle, or, in some cases, weren't even born yet. I have purposely stayed away from a reporter methodology in this book by deciding against that clinical approach to rehash fact gathering and endless impersonal interviews. There are a couple of people who are still alive from back then who haven't been sufficiently written about, and I do want you to get to know them better. Chris O'Dell was one, and now I want you to meet Jack Oliver. Here's a recent and rather orderly chat between two recovering scoundrels. Because I never thought to ask about his path to 3 Savile Row, I suggested he start from the beginning.

Jack tells me he was born in 1945 and grew up in Muswell Hill, about seven miles north of London, known for its hills, lush landscape, eighteenth century homes, chapels, and outstanding schools. Writers, academics, politicians, actors, business people, and even a few rockers came out of the picturesque place. Jack says he went to school with the likes of Ray and Dave Davies of the Kinks and iconic singer Rod Stewart, whose mother still lives there. And, like those talented blokes, music and art was in his blood at a very young age.

Jack attended art school and got his degree in design. He landed his first job right out of college at a King's Road Studio, which was the epicenter of 1960s London style and fashion. Every night after work, Jack hit the clubs with his friends and co-workers and hung out with a lot of people in the music business. Everybody in that industry seemed to love what they did, so Jack changed course and aimed his career in that direction. Through a friend, he got a job as an office boy at Chappell Publishing. He was twenty-one years old and making five pounds a week.

"I thought I was in the big time!" Jack chuckles at the memory.

Jack's hard work was rewarded with bigger and better jobs. He was assigned to a few small American publishing companies in the Deep South to see if he could sell songs. Despite not knowing a thing about our nation's Bible Belt, its people, or its unique culture, Jack performed well—he sold a lot of songs in a year's time.

"I was a sponge and I was young and wanted to get ahead. I stayed late everywhere I worked," Jack said. "I was friendly with a person named Gary Osborne, whose father was a big-time band leader. I was at their house a lot and met very many important people, paid my dues, and learned as I went along in the business."

Jack and I agree that, in most cases, it is advantageous to move into a major entertainment business market like London, LA, Nashville, or New York City to get a head start on a music "biz" dream. You need to work hard, make friends with like-minded people, and then be patient…hang out, hang in there, keep your eyes and ears open, and watch your back. If you keep your head down, your spirits up, and take every opportunity to learn your craft, time will become your friend, and when it comes to friends, years of faithful networking with colleagues will pay off. Someone in your circle of mates will eventually get a break and they bring their buddies along with them, because the deep bond that develops over the hard times is profound and lives long. Combine this with talent and paying dues and you are on your way. It's old school, it's the college of hard rocks and necessary knocks, and it's the street savvy way of getting ahead and staying there.

While Jack was getting to know everything about the back end of the business, the performance bug suddenly bit. He and friend Gary Osborne formed The Chocolate Watch Band in 1966 and shortly thereafter signed a deal with Decca, the same label that signed the Rolling Stones. Gary sang lead, Jack played bass, and they both wrote the songs.

The Chocolate Watch Band was the darling of pirate radio (about a dozen stations that broadcasted songs the BBC would not) and their two singles ("Requiem" and "The Sound of the Summer") did quite well. However, the UK government closed the international waters loophole that allowed these radio stations to operate through the Marine Broadcasting Offences Act of 1967, and Jack and Gary quickly realized they had no outlet for their songs. The government sank their bubbling offshore music careers with the stroke of a pen. Goodbye Decca, hello unemployment line.

Actually, Jack didn't stay unemployed that long. He went back to his boss at Chappell Publishing and asked for his old job back. It had been filled with Jack's departure, but his old boss did give him a tip, "There's a job opening at this new company…maybe there's something for you there."

At the appointed time, Jack showed up at a four-story office building at 94 Baker Street in London, the site of the short-lived Apple boutique and the street where fictional detective Sherlock Holmes lived in an apartment. Like Sherlock's sidekick, Jack became Apple's Watson and began building the elementary foundation there for his long tenure at the blossoming new enterprise.

"I go into this guy's office and it's all white." Jack smiles as he recalls that January 1968 day. "The paint on the wall was white, the carpets were white, and this white guy with a big afro and wearing a psychedelic suit was seated on a white leather couch. I sat on the other white leather couch while we chatted for a bit."

Jack was referring to Terry Doran who worked for a new company called Apple. At the time, the Beatles had not announced the formation of Apple or that they were structuring a new business venture, so everything was hush-hush. Terry was a former car dealer from Liverpool and a good friend of Brian Epstein's. (Terry has been widely rumored to be "the man in the motor trade" in the Beatles' "She's Leaving Home.") Even though Terry knew nothing about publishing, he was going to be running Apple's new publishing company. It would appear that, in the early stages of putting the cast and crew together for Apple, in many instances, knowing nothing about the job that a person was going to be doing did not seem to be a hindrance to getting employment there.

The conversation between Jack and Terry was genteel, polite, and strangely went nowhere. Jack knew nothing about this company or its players, only that it was a new publishing venture. Terry, in turn, didn't seem to know what he was doing. The conversation took a twist when Terry threw Jack a proverbial curveball by plainly announcing, "Well, I don't know what you can really do." Jack caught the curveball with a home-run smash of his own by turning it around on Terry.

"Well, it looks to me like you need an assistant, doesn't it?" Jack said, feeding his ego. He could see Terry's chest puff out in reaction to the flattery and could tell he liked the sound of that. After a few seconds, Terry asked him when he could start. "Tomorrow," was Jack's answer, and Jack was on board just like that.

But the story gets better...much better. Jack still had no idea who he was really working for, and on his first day of work Terry asked Jack if he wanted to attend MIDEM—an annual music festival and pop market that takes place in the south of France. "Yes, of course," he replied. The next day Jack flew to Cannes, was chauffeured to the five-star Carlton Hotel, and was taken to a large suite overlooking the Mediterranean Sea. Suddenly the doors opened and out walked Paul McCartney.

"Well now, this is a good job," Jack said to himself after the first day in France. I like this!

(I was going to write a brief chapter explaining how much fun it was working with the Beatles and being at Apple, but I realized Jack's story about his first days with the company will give you an idea of what it could be like at any given time.)

Jack spent the entire week with Paul and Terry, hanging out by the hotel pool, ogling European beauties in bikinis, ordering room service, attending lavish industry dinners, and hitting the clubs. Good job, indeed. But when Jack got back to London, he was all business, and when the offices moved to Savile Row, Jack later switched jobs and went to work in Derek Taylor's office. It was there he was assigned to manage artist Mary Hopkin, who was just eighteen at the time of her signing.

Mary's "Those Were the Days" was a worldwide smash in 1968 and came immediately on the heels of the Beatles' "Hey Jude." The one-two punch of these two singles announced to the record industry that Apple was a major player in this game. (Having two of our first four records make the top of England and America's music charts was phenomenal for a new record company. The odds of scoring a hit record places record labels' success ratio in an approximate 99 percent failure category. Batting 50 percent for openers was an amazing feat.)

Jack's management of Hopkin was just another facet of the industry he learned along the way, and it made him invaluable to Apple. My boss, Ron Kass, recognized Jack's worth and recruited him for the Apple Records division where he was bestowed a Head of Production title, and that's where Jack and I began forging a bond.

Besides all Jack's fun perks of working at 3 Savile Row, there was a lot of nut- and-bolts work that needed to be done, and a large amount of that work required coordinating with the US manager of Apple Records. Jack was my go-to man at Apple. He seemed to be a steady rock for me in the day-to-day rock pile of madness that surrounded him from every floor. Although most of the activity was centered on creativity and artistic innovation, there was always the mundane to deal with in terms of deadlines, graphics, coordination of assignments, and movement of materials between the UK and the US. Of course, adding in four bosses stirring the pot with divergent spoons made for a pretty volatile mixture. Jack helped steady the ship from his end, making my distant job more effective and cohesive. Jack eventually became president of Apple, but at that time he was the head of Apple International. Recently he jokingly revealed to me that the reason he and I spent so much time communicating with one another was because I was a foreigner and therefore was his responsibility.

America was the biggest market for their product, so a lot of initial promotion, merchandising, and marketing efforts were focused on my territory. The reason Jack and I got along so well from the get-go is that we were wired very much in the same way. As I mentioned earlier, we both were hard workers and took our jobs seriously. Jack was unique. He was an erratic calm in the center of a whimsical firestorm—a raging firestorm that needed to be tracked closely so it didn't get out of control. The Beatles creativity would light the place up and spark a lot of enthusiastic energy, but, in the midst of it all, stuff like album artwork needed to be put in boxes to be shipped somewhere, deadlines had to be met, and the American left hand needed to be up to speed with the British right hand. I mentioned we were wired alike, but all the wires weren't tied to the hard work wagon. There were some that led right to where the local nightlife was happening the hottest. They say all work and no play makes Jack a dull boy. Well, let me put it this way...Jack was one of the sharpest guys I ever met.

All this reminiscing led us to the topic of *Let It Be* and the rooftop concert. He recalls the boys "weren't getting on too well" with a lot of bickering in the Apple offices and on the set of the film. He was privy to some of the conversations about where the final concert should take place. He recalls two locations: the Sahara Desert and the London Palladium. The former was a logistical nightmare and the latter simply didn't work out for various reasons. When the rooftop was suggested a few days before the actual filming, Jack thought it was a brilliant idea.

"There was a lot of talk about the roof not being safe and that it was going to collapse," Jack said. "I've always found it interesting that no one actually thought to hire an engineer to look at it and say, 'You might not want to put too many people up there because it might collapse.' It was a bit of a worry, and that's one of the reasons why they limited the amount of people up there." But that nonchalance and "make it up as you go" attitude was what made Apple...Apple. It was emblematic of the company's wild, roll the dice attitude about almost everything, and that's what made it fun and exciting.

I asked Jack what his duties entailed in preparation for the concert. His answer was immediate and I could still sense a tinge of frustration around its edges.

"I was a cop for a day," he answers wryly. "I was working nonstop, going up and down the stairs, trying to stop people from going up there while dashing back and forth between the reception area and the roof. I was just running all the time, just trying to keep it together."

I remember seeing Jack popping in and out the door to the roof, but unfortunately his movements were never filmed. Jack puts it this way, "No one ever caught any pictures of me on the roof that day, nothing to seal my infamy. It was a magic moment in history, and the rooftop was the crowning glory of my time at Apple...and I was there."

Well, that was then and this is now, and here we are once again involved in a film being made, but this time it is about the Beatles and Apple...and us. Because Jack is the producer, he will make sure we are both in it. We are older now so there are no stairs, and we are purposely doing my segment in Florida where the weather is warm and sunny. And, instead of being hard at work, we take a lot of breaks because it's hard to work when the gulf waters await and it is...warm and sunny.

A is for Apple, B is for Beach!

GENTLE GIANT

It is very hard for me to write about Mal Evans, but if I am to tell of my experiences with the Beatles, London, Apple, 3 Savile Row, or the roof, there is something deep inside that says it would be impossible to do so without including Mal. But as I attempted to write about him for this book, even after decades since his passing, it became so painful that I have opted for including what I wrote a long time ago. The fact that we did share the experience of the roof had the feeling of being simply appropriate due to the depth of our friendship. Because our relationship began in London with the Beatles, it was logical that such a bonding moment was meaningful as we carried forth into California and the years beyond all that. On the preceding pages, I have been covering events and revisiting the days of Apple and the Beatles, but I insert this reflection because I want to end my story with the best part by telling you about a person...Malcom Frederick Evans.

I truly loved Mal. I had never met anyone like him. We developed a friendship and a deep loyalty that I never expect to experience again with another person. We met and that was it—pals. I believe that Mal guided me safely down the narrow corridors and tight chambers of that proverbial yellow submarine and guaranteed me smooth sailing with his four captains. His verbalized acceptance, approval, and his trust of me was passionately imparted to the Beatles, and this, I believe, helped give me immediate and confident acceptance on their part. Many times, I would test the waters with Mal before approaching one of them on a business matter.

He was the first person who became a deep and true friend when I entered the Beatles empire—I was possibly the last friend to talk to him before he was killed.

Mal was a big, lovable, soft-spoken, gentle giant of a man. I'll never forget a time in October 1968 when he and I took Jackie Lomax on an Apple tour of the United States to promote the album and a single that George Harrison had produced. (At that time only the single "Sour Milk Sea" was released.) As it was one of our first Apple releases, and one of George's first productions, we knew it was important to do a good job. Mal was the consummate road manager and treated Jackie with the same respect and care that he afforded the Beatles. Jackie, Mal, and I had hung out, partied, and shared a casual relationship, until we took Jackie on the road. Then things changed. Jackie was now elevated to star status in Mal's mind and that was the way he was to be treated while we were touring. Jackie's every wish and desire was taken care of—no different than if he were John Lennon, Paul McCartney, George Harrison, or Ringo Starr. Mal expected me to act accordingly. I set up the promotional itinerary and Mal set up all the incidentals. He preceded Jackie's every move whether it was walking in front of him down a radio station hallway or going ahead to curbside at the hotel to make sure the limo was indeed waiting. Jackie was always able to go straight from his room into the waiting car without having to suffer the inconvenience of being a star left waiting in a hotel lobby. As with the Beatles, when Mal was in attendance, he was everywhere at once taking care of everything.

I remember one night in Cleveland when we spent the evening at a local rock club with the music director, disc jockey, and station manager of the main Top 40 station there. We were sitting at a table along a railing that bordered the walkway through the middle of the club. Our table was in a section that was elevated about a foot-and-a-half higher than the floor of the walkway. Mal was sitting next to Jackie and was turned away, with his back to him while he was engaged in deep conversation with the disc jockey about Jackie's record, when a strange thing happened. Jackie and I were seated across from each other at the end of the table near the walkway, hanging over the railing and watching the activity in the club while the next act was setting up. Suddenly, a scruffy young guy appeared, got right in Jackie's face, and started picking a fight with what he figured was this skinny little wimp with long black hair and a sissy-type proper accent and all. Mal's finely tuned radar sensed something was awry with his artist in this very noisy club and, in one motion, raised up out of his chair, turned around, and with the added advantage of the foot-and-a-half riser was suddenly hovering over this obnoxious little twit.

I only knew Mal's loving and kind side, and, until this night, I had never seen a scarier look on a man's face or a man look any bigger than Mal did when he unfolded that big body out of his chair and, like a raging blowfish, doubled in size. Simultaneously with his repositioning, Mal let out the loudest roar three inches away from and directly into the twit's face. There was no conversation or male posturing, or even face saving. I am sure the agitator made a record-breaking situation evaluation because either he disappeared magically or immediately made a faster-than-the-speed-of-light exit out of the immediate area. Mal stood transfixed for a few long moments just to make sure no more trouble would enter our space, and then he quietly sat down and returned to his conversation. What I remember most happened a few seconds later. Mal turned back around to Jackie, softly patted him on the arm, gave him a warm look as if to say, "Everything's okay; Mal's here," and then resumed his conversation. When I think of Mal, it is that kind, gentle look I see on his face. Of all the times we shared, I think I have chosen to remember him that way.

The promo tour was a success. The record and Jackie Lomax were not.

Of course, George was concerned about the record and the tour. He therefore kept in touch with us all during the trip. He surprised us by picking us up at LAX when we flew in after the tour was over. It was so ordinary. He met us at the gate, and the four of us fell in step, talking nonstop all the way out to the car. Nobody noticed us. We were all very tired but went to George's rented house that evening and listened to music until late into the night.

I knew Mal outside of Apple. I knew Lil, his wife. She and Mal and their kids came to LA and stayed at my house after the Beatles broke up. The youngsters were thrilled to be there. I was recently divorced and lived alone in a large secluded house in the Hollywood Hills with a giant swimming pool, and everything was so California, just like they had seen in the movies. The weather was sunny and incredible all the time they were there, and Mal's kids looked like prunes at the end of each day from spending so much time in the water.

Mal and Lil eventually separated. When he came to live in LA, I was in the outlaw mode with Waylon Jennings, et al., and so Mal and I became the Englishman and the cowboy riding hard herd on the Sunset Strip until the sun came up many mornings. Mal had a rough time in LA, and things were not going well for quite a long time. His life was much different now compared to the nonstop excitement living in the center of the Beatles world in London so, unfortunately, in California his spirits would get uplifted and then hopes dashed with projects that kept falling apart. There were too many let downs and too few let's rock.

I was sitting home late one afternoon in January 1976 working at my tape deck editing a sequence for an album I had just produced. I had a next-day deadline, and to make matters more pressing, that night was the Billboard Awards Show. Jessi Colter was up for "New Female Country Artist of the Year" based on her hit record I had produced entitled "I'm Not Lisa." As Jessi's producer, I had been asked to accept for her in the event she won because she was on the road and couldn't attend.

Final album sequences are often hard for producers, and I was deep into my work when my phone rang. I answered, and it was Mal. I asked him how he was doing, and he started rambling on about how well everything was going. Something seemed peculiar, even though he was professing optimism, so in the middle of his good news I asked him what was wrong. "Nothing is wrong," he said and continued, "Paul and I just worked out some problems, and he is going to give me credit for some of the things I wrote with him…" I interrupted again, asking him what was wrong. "Nothing," he continued, "and besides that, I am signing a production deal with Atlantic Records and my book is going great, and because you were left out of other books, I am making sure you are all over it and…" I knew Mal too well and for too long, and somewhere beneath all this good news I sensed something I had never felt with Mal before.

Something was horribly wrong.

"Mal…Mal," I said. "Stop and listen to me for a second. Something's wrong, isn't it?" There was silence on his end. "We need to talk, don't we?" I asked. Momentary silence.

"Yes," he said softly.

"Mal, I can't meet you now because I have to leave for the awards show in a little while, but can we get together later tonight or first thing tomorrow for lunch?"

"Not tonight," he replied.

"How about I'll meet you tomorrow for lunch at Musso & Franks, okay? Okay, Mal?"

"Yeah, okay."

"One o'clock?"

"Sure."

"Fine, Mal. I'll see you then."

***

"…and the new female country artist of the year is…Jessi Colter. Accepting for Jessi is her producer, Ken Mansfield." Those were the words I heard that night, but they were way off in the distance and deep in an echo chamber. I could see the words coming out of comedian Flip Wilson's mouth as if in slow motion, and the trophy in his hand was a diffused blob. Just prior to the announcement, Diane Bennett, a friend and social columnist for the Hollywood Reporter, had come up to me. She put her arm around my shoulder and said, "I am sorry about Mal, Ken."

I turned quickly, "What do you mean…about Mal?"

"I thought you knew," she said uncomfortably. "He's been shot."

Flip was extending the award in my direction, and I was ushered on stage walking in a half-turned position facing Diane. I took the award out of his hand, "Mumble, mumble," and immediately headed back into the audience and to Diane's side.

"Is he okay?" I asked her, and she gave me the shorthand version. He was dead.

Harry Nilsson filled me in later with the details. He told me that it seemed Mal had become increasingly despondent that night. He was staying with his girlfriend, Fran Hughes, in a rented duplex near LA's Farmers Market, and had taken a gun upstairs and locked himself in the bedroom. Fran was afraid he was going to do something crazy and so she called the police to protect him from himself. There were several versions of what happened, but I chose to go with Harry's description of what went down. Four LAPD officers walked up to the bedroom, kicked the door open, saw the gun and shot him several times to keep him from hurting himself! Ironically, Mal was an honorary sheriff of Los Angeles County.

There is that part in all of us that always wants to make us feel guilty or responsible for the death of someone we are close to. For some reason, I can't pin that dragon on myself even though I was strategically positioned in this event. I think it is because I loved him too much to knowingly do anything to harm him, or to not be there if I thought he needed me. I also know in my heart that Mal would never blame me. These were crazy times, and we were all pretty much one pork chop short of a mixed grill. Time and events seemed to drift in and out of reality at their own given pace. Sometimes we would hop aboard our wild horses and ride like blazing daredevils on the frighteningly fast track we had inherited with the notoriety of it all. Sometimes our ride would stumble, and we would fall off. It was funny at first because we were young and invincible. We would jump up laughing, dust ourselves off, and leap back into the fray full force, unabashed and unblinking. The problem is that the ride kept getting faster, and the destination became more and more obscure.

Sometimes we would fall off and not even know it.

Mal fell when I wasn't looking.

EPILOGUE

I WENT INTO A DREAM

I am back on the roof of the old Apple building at 3 Savile Row in London's financial district and it is fifty years later, given a time lapse, a flashback, or a déjà vu or two. So much has gone down, gone askew in thought from both inside and outside this weathered, vain man's frozen stance. I breathe in the rush of decades past as I try to capture fleeting memories of this treasured space. I open my eyes slowly, like a surreal Fellini fade in to what surrounds me, and for the first time I can see clearly from where I stand, not only physically but also spiritually. I find myself transitionally transfixed looking out over a vaguely familiar portion of a timeless London skyline. My position becomes anchored when I notice the glass house on the building next door is still there. Things start coming back, but I sense it all has more to do with a going away.

I am scant minutes away from Carnaby Street, where I bought my hip English duds in the '60s. I am perched just illusionary footsteps away from Piccadilly Circus and from the clubs, the posh hotels, the four Beatles, and their running mates. A spatial Rolling Stone's throw from all those moves and all the bits and pieces that had so much to do with the shaping of my life later on. Good things, bad things, senseless things, important things, happening things…"things" being the operative word here.

I have revisited this spot as the concluding stopover on my return to the last time the music died. The reason I close my eyes so much as I stand here, whether in mind, body, or spirit, is because when they are closed, the echoes of that time ring so much louder and clearer as they make their way to my heart. After traveling so many miles over the years seeking recreation, recapture, and refreshment, I now realize I never expected to find redemption in this journey. I had been mistakenly looking for an abstract homecoming in the mechanics of a return visit, not a perspective on a final destination.

The time is one o'clock in the afternoon, approximately the same time of day I gathered here, with an incredibly small but extraordinarily bizarre flock of unruly angels five decades ago. With unrelenting majesty Rock 'n' Roll's rocking royalty, roadies, and regulars reverberated forth for the last time a lively litany of earth-shaking sounds and sensations from this place. If, as a writer, I was just looking for a poetic springboard, maybe I should have traveled here on April 29, 2002, so it would have been thirty-three and one third years later, just to put everything into a complete retrospective spin. But, I have lived this long with this time and place clinging to my cerebral coattails, and a sip of life's fine remembrance wine needed more time.

I am stopped in my tracks by the sudden realization that I have journeyed so far, aiming at, circling around, and zeroing in on this singular moment. Like Moses, after years of wandering in a desert, I have been led to a specific place for a divine purpose. In the spirit, I have been brought to the top of the mountain to hear from my Father God—just the two of us. It was time to stop having idle conversations and to be still and listen. I am reminded that He has filled my collection plate with sweet offerings of wisdom from faithful friends, passionate pastors, essential enemies, career cohorts, assorted acquaintances, and colorful characters of my past—wonderful people who placed golden contributions into my outstretched soul. After many years of pressing in to my Creator's heart, I sense there is something timeless in the wind that is blowing up from the historical street below.

This is just a building, this is just a town, that was just an event, and unfortunately, in some ways, I have returned to this place just a little less confused than I was then. I was dealing with the shallow importance of worldly things in those heady days, and the dilemmas I've experienced in my travels since then have always had to do with not letting go of those same old terrestrial considerations. I am immediately made aware of this skewered perspective—a revelation adeptly accompanied by the unwelcome news that, for decades, a part of me has refused to change.

None of what is beginning to take place in this moment of introspection minimizes the incredible event that took place here a half a century ago…it has more to do with my importance shrinking in comparison. The sudden and unexpected realization that I had developed a sophisticated lack of trust in God's ability to do a better job with my life brings about a peculiar sense of awkwardness to this moment. I was fed many meals, a partaker of rampant feasts of phenomenal moments in my life. Indeed, in worldly terms, my story is about "a lucky man who made the grade." God continuously filled my cup to the brim until it was overflowing with blessings, and then I would walk away, without leaving a grateful tip of my hat or even giving thanks for the many blessings in life like the one that happened here.

I am ready to start running from what is beginning to unfold on this roof, but I am aware within a matter of a few feet I will become airborne if I do. I just need to make all this stuff less a part of me. That's what it is all about. It was not about the trials, the pain, the disappointments, the failures, or the downward slide. It definitely is not about the hit records, the fame, the money, the stars, the exciting tours, or even the immutably appointed or pointless times in my life. No, it has always been about the other part, the new part, the part that leaves the old part behind, the part that has a fresh beginning, the part that is about Him and not me.

The din from the street below created by the big city's lunchtime multitudes roars up into my awareness and startles me into the realization I am the only one standing in this place right now—a lonely misguided soul. Perceptively paralyzed, I self-interrogate, asking how I could even imagine recreating or recouping anything out of this moment with the ground rules I had established. My thoughts are rushing now; my wits are in a whirlwind. They begin crowding the strained edges of my mind, as the law of emotional centrifugal force gains momentum and memorial speed—stirred up debris from my past is wildly scraping against the edge of a thrashed consciousness.

I will admit that when I opened the door leading out to that gritty vista and walked out onto the roof, I had an overwhelming sense that not only was I going to feel a rush of cold air but that I would be hit flat in the face with warm memories, solid rim shots, and the strains of "Get Back."

I expected Paul to turn around and smile at me through that beard I never liked, nodding his head to the side as if to say, "Hey, great, look, we're all here. It's just us and it still feels good." I still wonder how he could feel good in that cold weather dressed in just a suit.

I picture John staring into space, leaning into the microphone with his long hair flowing in the rooftop winds. The fur coat he was wearing might not have been his, but the song he was singing was.

I can see Ringo looking out and beyond the backs of his mates, appearing almost alone in the backline of the band, very noticeable in his shiny red coat. Like an old friend, he was where he belonged...backing up his mates.

And George would still be bent over his guitar checking on his frozen fingers to make sure that they are in the right place. His black fur coat couldn't cover everything, but he was the only one who came dressed for the cold occasion.

On that day, January 30, 1969, four idealistic, long-time friends had no idea they were saying goodbye to a monumental era in music history, and ushering in a change in the bond and deep friendship that would never have the same boyhood street passion that had anointed their music for so many years. The last song of the set on the roof that day, "Get Back," proclaimed the end of a beginning no one was really ready to accept. The local Londoners heard it on the streets below; yes, a crowd of people stood and stared, unaware of a reluctant reverberation pouring forth that would never die—an eerie echo wafted out and over the rooftop railings that incredible day and still resonates in the hearts of those who remember.

I know now how monumental that day was in my life, and because of such incredible successes and events at such a young age, I know I peaked too high and too soon. A pinnacle of that magnitude, happening so early in my pleasure-seeking life, dominated everything that followed. A milestone became a millstone. It became a shifty idol that I worshiped without realizing and became a point that I had been unable to go beyond.

I am not diminishing the recent stops on this long trek, and I must make it crystal clear I am not even suggesting the incredible reflections I experienced on the way were not immensely important and downright mind boggling at times. In fact, I am identifying this roof as a critical spot—the top of a long, steep climb. We only spend a minute there at the very top of the world's world. Most of our time is spent going up and down the mountain, and that is the part I need to focus on.

I look out and see everything for the first time. I soared through this period in my life picking up worldly possessions and lifelong impressions. Then one day, everything seemed to fall apart and I had to get rid of "stuff" in order to move on. I discovered the homes, cars, and prized possessions were the easy things to lose. It's the baggage I had unknowingly gathered along the darkened way that clung to my walk like grass stains that wouldn't wash out. It isn't the things that were the problem; it was the nothings. It's that feeling of passing through life, collecting worthless junk while leaving very little of permanent value behind.

I look out from this place and I can see forever. Forever…that is the where, why, what, and mainly "Who" it is eventually all about. Forever evolves into eternity and I know the journey has ended here.

That cold January day has always been one of the biggest days in my life. Now I look around and I discover it is just a dirty old roof. I look away from the roof and there is forever. I look back at the roof and it looks even smaller than it did a few moments ago. As I stand frozen in place by these cold facts, I realize these reflections and a warm jacket are already more than I am going to leave this life with.

I can actually sense God smiling up at me from the street below, laughing across the ledges of the surrounding buildings, in rhythm with the banging door I left open behind me when I came out into this moment. I can tell He is thrilled that I finally got it. His imagined amusement expands into a genuine laugh of incredulous celestial disbelief that it took me so long. Yet, it is in His way of gentle grace we both know we can finally get it on. I don't need to get back; I need to get going. It is all so very simple. It's just so hard to be simple.

I drift down and out of the building and merge out and away from that manmade structure onto a street of gold. I stand with my back to the building and turn my head slowly as I look up and down Savile Row reimagining my journey in and out of this dream. I cherish both the then of this experience and the future that lies ahead. I know now this journey actually started long before I set out, and will end in eternity with Him. I finally became a man today because I realized it is all about just being His child. My dad was right…you can see Colorado from here, or wherever you stand, but I still believe it does matter which way you are facing.

There is no need to travel back to any of the other places from that period. I feel emptied out and filled up at the same time. All these mountains of words I have poured forth on these pages, and in this journey back in time, become a heap of torn clippings blowing away in the wind. Solomon nailed it when he said our vain efforts are of no import now. I had no bags when I left on this trip and in returning I have ended up with even less baggage. Thanks for tagging along.

The dream is over. I had communion today and it wasn't necessary to come here to be here.

But I just had to look.

Peace and His love

Ken Mansfield
Former US Manager Apple Records

Itinerary for Mr. Stanley Gortikov - President of Capitol Records Inc.

Saturday 10th August

7.40 - London Airport - Arrival met by Ron Kass

Driven to Royal Lancaster Hotel, Bayswater Road.
Check into suite no: 1727
Peter Brown will be there to greet you
Ron and Peter will leave you to enable you to have a short rest.

13.00 hrs - Rolls Royce will pick you and Ken Mansfield & Larry Delaney
up and take you to Ritz Hotel for lunch with four Beatles,
Neil Aspinall, Mal Evans, Ron Kass and Peter Brown.

14.30 hrs. - Paul McCartney has to leave to keep an appointment in
the recording studios, the rest of the party will then go to the
new Apple Offices at 3, Savile Row, where Alexis Mardas (head of
Electronics division) and Derek Taylor (Apple Records publicist)
will be waiting.   After introduction, we will play you some
Beatle material which is scheduled for the new album.
A buffet tea will be served during the afternoon.

20.00 hrs - The Rolls Royce will pick-up you Ken and Larry from the
Royal Lancaster Hotel and go to the Queens Theatre to see a comedy
"Half Way Up the Tree" starring Robert Morley, directed by
Sir John Gielgud and written by Peter Ustinov.
The theatre party will comprise of John Lennon, Yoko, Neil Aspinall &
Susie, Ron Kass and Peter Brown.

23.00 - Dinner at the Club dell'Aretusa, 107, Kings Road.
Where the party will be joined by, Paul McCartney and Peter Asher.

Sunday 11th August

We have purposely left this day open specific arrangements can be
made during our discussions on Saturday, and we have ear-marked
the day for "ideas". A good time to start the day would probably
be brunch at 13.00 in the Royal Lancaster.

Internal 1968 Apple document, probably written by Barbara O'Donnell,
outlining the schedule for our visit to 3 Savile Row where Capitol and
Apple execs would begin setting up the Apple label launch in America.
Sunday's itinerary was not defined like Saturday's but that was the day we
really got a lot of business taken care of.

Feb 10 1969

Dear George:

By now Ken Mansfield has communicated my decision to pass release rights on the "King of Fuh" single, but I wanted personally to communicate my complete rationale. First, I find the record itself delightful, whimsical, and a funny spoof on one of my favorite words. It is cleverly done and certainly is not personally offensive to me.
But I am not "Mr Average American" who constitutes our market — whether he be retailer, wholesaler, youth purchaser, or parent of youth purchaser.

If you are interested in the release of King of Fuh I would readily waive rights so that you could place it with another record company and would cooperate in any possible way, even though I jealously and selfishly deplore any non-Capitol Beatles/Apple relationships within the US.

However, I do urge you to abandon such release plans. In the public press, and therefore, in the public image, the Beatles too often, too unfairly have recently been the victim of distortion. You don't deserve to by typified as proponents of a "public be damned" philosophy which too many are prone to tag you with. I respect you too much to be comfortable with having you exposed to still another opportunity for public censure. So little can be gained, and the backlash potential is so great.

The commercial potential of the "King of Fuh" will have several critical limitations, some akin to those experienced by the Two Virgins album. The record will not be airplayed; radio stations will be too sensitive over their own public image, parental criticism, and possible complaints to the Federal Communications Commission. many retailers, and wholesalers, responsive to negative adult consumer reaction, will refrain from stocking the single. They would be responsive to the many parents who simply don't want to hear the F word coming over the phonographs on their 12 year-old daughters. Despite these restrictions, the record may sell well, particularly through "underground" interest.

Of course, purveyors of the single will run legal risks in certain geographical areas similar to those encountered by the Two Virgins, such as confiscations and sale injunctions where local "obscenity" laws prevail. Those don't bother me, but two other legal influences are most vital:

1. The mailed shipment of phonograph records in the US enjoys a preferential postal rate, constantly under attack in Congress. The defense of the rate is rooted in many phonograph records being cultural and educational. Critics constantly support their views with examples of those records which they typify as being in "bad taste", and the "King of Fuh" single would most likely be selected as an example.

2. A strong effort is being made by Capitol and other key record companies to secure from radio stations public performance income for artists, musicians, and record manufacturers, this payment to be derived for records being played on commercial programs over the air. Opponents of the move are prone, as above, to single out "questionable" lyrics as rationale for undermining efforts to place this legislation under the protection of our copyright statutes.

You, both as The Beatles and as individuals, have created a mystique and charisma that is unique. You refresh it all the time, and millions identify with you. I maintain that "King of Fuh" imperils rather than enhances a great portion of that rapport you have so successfully built. What possibly can be accomplished by antagonizing the "squares" who own our radio stations, operate our retail outlets, and serve as parents of the millions whom you constantly delight? Yes, even without the "King of Fuh", you retain infinite capacities and opportunities to innovate and to counter the sometimes indefensible morality patterns of society in the US.

That's my cue to close now …

Stan

Content copy of a letter from Stanley Gortikov to George Harrison, John Lennon, Paul McCartney, Ringo Starr with cc to Peter Asher, Neil Aspinall, Ron Kass, Ken Mansfield. It was addressed to George but intended for the four Beatles. Stanley includes personal asides and comments to the Beatles which I have chosen to leave out for his privacy. I have reprinted this portion of his dialogue to show how Stan had my back concerning the King of Fuh record, how hands on he was in this situation and also to illustrate how complex our job could be at times.

TO: APPLE CORPS DISTRIBUTION LIST

FROM: KEN MANSFIELD

DATE: AUGUST 22, 1969

CHART POSITIONS

Singles:	Billboard	Cash Box
"GIVE PEACE A CHANCE"	15	11
"THAT'S THE WAY GOD PLANNED IT"	65	74

Albums:		
THE BEATLES	67	51

SALES

Singles:

#1808 - Billy Preston - "That's The Way God Planned It"	101,900
#1809 - Plastic Ono Band - "Give Peace A Chance"	756,700

Albums:

ST 3354 - Jackie Lomax - "Is This What You Want"	28,100
ST 3357 - John Lennon/Yoko Ono - "Life With The Lions"	58,900
ST 3358 - George Harrison - "Electronic Sounds"	39,700

Regards,

Ken

Ken Mansfield

KM: ja

Goodbye lovely people !!!!

Ken

As far as I know this was my last written correspondence to Apple before leaving to join Ron Kass at MGM Records. It looks like I said goodbye with a status report on our current projects.

MGM RECORDS

DIVISION OF METRO-GOLDWYN-MAYER INC., 9255 Sunset Boulevard, Los Angeles, California 90069

October 8, 1969

Mr. Ringo Starr
Brookfields
Cut Mill Lane
Elstead, Surrey,
England

Dear Ringo:

After living on Abbey Road for the last two weeks, I just had to drop you a line to tell you how much the new album gasses me. Needless to say, hearing this great new product and not being directly involved with it was a little sad for me.

My new thing with MGM is great and working with Ron Kass again and rebuilding this label is extremely rewarding.

I have enclosed a copy of a record I thought you might enjoy. To say the least, it is an unusual version of "Hey Jude." The producer is Roger Karshner, who is with Capitol Records and the artist is billed as "the Far Out, Acid Rock, Underground Feet of Harry Zonk." It's a rock & roll tap-dance version of "Hey Jude" and, as Roger says, "Harry Zonk will dance his way to your mind." I hope you get as big a kick out of it as I did as it is a far cry from the record I first heard sitting on the floor of a large room at 3 Savile Row over a year ago.

The best of everything. Hope to see you in London soon.

Love & Apples,

Ken Mansfield

KM: ja

It is obvious that I missed my friends in the U.K. This was sent to Ringo's home only 6 weeks after leaving Apple.

And then there was Mal....

mgm records ken
mansfield director
of exploitation 9255
sunset blvd suite 625
los angeles 69 calif
phone (213) 276-2244

Nov 20, 1969

Dear Mal:

I've never written a fan letter before but feel moved to do so now. This is not a fan letter of normal sorts as it is not directed to a person or an act but instead is aimed at a concept and those that make up the heart and soul of that concept.

The Beatles, the apple thing and those of you who are honestly _with_ the Beatles comprise a beautiful center of magnetic warmth out of which is generated a desire to do truly great things. A sadness lies in how screwed up things can get when the "impure in heart" get their hands on it.

During this last trip I sensed so much frustration and discontent from *many of you but it didn't hit me until after I had got on the plane to Rome. It's amazing that this can happen when things really don't have to be that way --- especially when the victims of this discontent deserve a much better state of being.*

I don't know why I am writing all of this --- maybe it is just to say I care; that my association with you and the others is very dear to me and that I am always here to help out in any way possible.

Be good -- Be happy - Be!!

Love and Apples

Ken

mgm records ken
mansfield director
of exploitation 9255
sunset blvd suite 625
los angeles 69 calif
phone (213) 276-2244

This was a very personal and emotional letter. Instead of dictating to my secretary I wrote it in my own handwriting. There was another handwriting…on the wall, as it's said, and a big part of my decision to follow Kass to MGM. I returned to London for a couple of days just three months after leaving Apple and could see how everything had changed in that short time. It was what I sensed. Mal had kept this and a copy was sent to me many years later by a mutual friend.

MGM RECORD CORPORATION, 7165 Sunset Boulevard, Los Angeles, California 90046 – (213) 874–0180

KEN MANSFIELD
VICE PRESIDENT/DIRECTOR
MARKETING AND ARTISTS DEVELOPMENT

November 23, 1970

Mr. Mal Evans
135 Staines Road, East
Sunbury On Thames
Middlesex, England

Dear Mal:

Let this be my first fan letter to you. I can't tell
you how happy and excited I was for you when I first
heard the Badfinger record (an obvious smash). It's nice
to know that the good guys do win once in awhile. Along
the lines of hero worshipping, I finally had a chance to
hear some of George's new stuff and it's fantastic!
Please pass this on to George as I know he's dying for
my opinion.

Hopefully, I will be in London in December. Please let
me know immediately if you are going to be out of town
any time in December. I'll try to give you a call before
I come over so we can set things up.

Love and Apples,

Ken Mansfield

KM: ja

KEN MANSFIELD
PRESIDENT

November 3, 1972

Mr. Mal Evans
135 Staines Road, East
Sunbury on Thames
Middlesex, England

Dear Mal,

Thought I'd let you see what I'm doing over here by sending you my
first album releases since I have taken over Barnaby. It seems
like it has been so long since we have talked to each other that
it's almost impossible to try to cover all the things that have
happened in a letter. I guess I'll just wait until I come over
for Midem, and we'll spend a couple of days just "doing it up."

You are constantly in my mind though, as you left two pairs of
your giant size socks in the laundry room, which I occasionally
use for Lisa and Mark's sleeping bags when we go camping. Hope
you like the albums -- the Hagers' is dedicated especially to you.

Love and apples,

Ken Mansfield

KM:lp

Enc.

BARNABY
RECORDS 816 N. LA CIENEGA BLVD., LOS ANGELES, CALIF. 90069, (213) 657-6150

My friendship with Mal was deep and personal. He and his family would
stay at my Hollywood Hills home for extended periods. His wife Lil loved
the bougainvillea there and the kids couldn't stay out of the pool—an unusual treat for them. They looked like shriveled prunes by days end. Mal
eventually joined me in Hollywood.

Neil Aspinall seated at his desk in his second-floor office. Neil's overwhelming stature at Apple and this picture suggests who was actually running things at 3 Savile Row. Photo by Tommy Hanley.

Paul McCartney and Apple president Ron Kass deep in conversation in Ron's ground floor office. Gentle Mal Evans, as always, was nearby ready to jump into action on a moment's notice. To me, Mal and Neil were the heart and grit of Apple. Photo by Tommy Hanley.

Apple

Dear Ken re. Life with the Lions

We'd like the Zapple label to be SILVER not white — it more subtle! o.k?

also it must be out sooner x than June 2nd. Yoko and I hope to be there (N.Y.) MAY 26th. — don't spread it round (too much) until you hear from Derek Taylor.

7. MAY 15th — U. CAN DO IT!

love, John + Yoko xx

Apple Corps Ltd., 3 Savile Row, London, W.1., 01-734 8232. Cables Apicore London, W.1. Director, N. S. Aspinall.

This handwritten letter by John Lennon was mailed to me at the Hollywood Capitol/Apple offices the first week in May 1969. It includes a self-portrait line drawing of he and Yoko on original Apple stationery. It is one of the only known personal documents written by Lennon concerning his pet project, the Zapple label. He was intimately involved and available to further the project. Of special interest is the additional Apple/Zapple historical aspect of his request to change the label color and Lennon shorthand (rond for round, U for you), or simply misspelling.

John sent this "one of the first" copies of the "Life with the Lions" album to me but I didn't notice he had signed it. Overrun with thousands of LPs in later years I began unloading most of them at a used record shop in San Francisco's Noe Valley district. As the buyer for the store was restacking the piles of records, "Life with the Lions" ended this side up on top of one of the stacks where I noticed John's handwritten note for the first time. I immediately retrieved it and returned the twenty-five cents they had paid me for the album.

I was positioned to George's right at this 1965 *Help!* Hollywood press conference. Capitol president Alan Livingston is at their left and Capitol exec Buck Stapleton is behind me. This was my first time working with the Beatles. I occupied the same position during their 1966 press conference also held in Capitol's Hollywood Studio A. (See www.fabwhitebook.com, *The White Book*.) I would never ask for a photo with the Beatles so our photographer took a shot from this angle to give me a personal pic with the lads.

I would receive signed albums from Apple London unsolicited. I have a suspicion it was either Mal Evans or Jack Oliver who "helped" getting this one.

This photo was taken in 1965 and was my first day working with British bands. I picked up Peter and Gordon at the airport and witnessed first-hand the frenzy taking place around the British invasion artists. Gordon Waller is signing autographs and I'm on the far left, behind the police escort. Keith "Avo" Avison, their tour manager, is behind me. Peter Asher was just off camera to the other side.

All pictures on this page are from Ken Mansfield's personal archive.

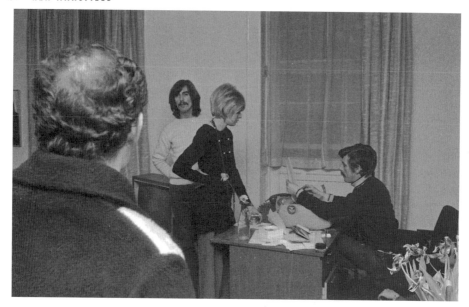

George Harrison, Chris O'Dell, and Derek Taylor. Not sure whose office they were using but it wasn't Derek, Chris or George's so you can tell how casual day-to-day activities were by this photo. Photo by Tommy Hanley.

Lots of activity always going on in Derek Taylor's third floor office. That's Mary Hopkin posing for a publicity photo in Derek's famous wicker chair. The girl far left is staffer Carol Paddon. Derek Taylor is lighting a cigarette and staffer Mavis Smith is on the right. The photographer and his assistant unknown. Photo by Tommy Hanley.

Apple's chief executive Ron Kass and Capitol Records President Stanley Gortikov were my greatest teachers and influences in all matters concerning life in the music industry. To follow Kass to MGM was an honor but to leave serving under Gortikov was a hard decision. The writing was on the wall concerning the eventual Beatles breakup and MGM was an exciting challenge. I also liked being a VP for the first time. Apple's Peter Asher and Mike O'Connor also joined us there. This is my favorite picture of Ron and me in our heyday.

DATEBOOK

Publishing Director/JEAN RAMER
Art Director/CHRISTINE DI NAPOLI
Associate Editor/FRANCES KIZERE
British Correspondent/GEORGE TREMLETT

VOL. 7, NO. 6

MGM Records, on the verge of packing it in after losses in the super-millions, has made a courageous last-stand effort. They have replaced their long-time power-people with (a) Ron Cass, (b) Peter Asher, (c) Ken Mansfield. All three were with Apple in the states or England and here's hoping they can perform some major miracles. Too bad they (MGM) didn't try transfusing some of the new blood before the dying company had reached corpse-like proportions.

I went to see Elvis Presley in Las Vegas and if he wasn't a gas! I had never seen him in person, him being slightly before my time, and I really dug him. He didn't do any of the hip-swinging, dang it all, but he did a great job on a lot of his old and new songs. And wow, he earned a cool million (after taxes, I hear) for a month's engagement. (For that kind of money, I'd be engaged to Jack The Ripper.)

Elvis recorded a live album during his month in L.V., and also I would imagine this is the beginning of the World Tour he wants to do as soon as possible.

The San Francisco Wild West Show, which was to be a partly-free partly-ticketed series of pop concerts, has been called off. Frankly, professional agitators came in from New York and started threatening the backers of the show and attacking the performers for participating in such a commercial venture. Finally, everyone involved just threw up their hands and quit trying.

Fuzz interrupted Delaney & Bonnie & Friends concert.

Hope the coming-up Big Sur Music Festival (slated to present Joan Baez, Joni Mitchel, Crosby-Stills-Nash & Young, etc.) doesn't meet with the same fate. Joan Baez, by the way, has a wonderful book out (it's in paperback) called "Daybreak." It's really beautiful and more than worth reading.

Everyone is talking about a group called Area Code 615 which is made up of ten session musicians from Nashville. Six of them have purportedly been with Dylan since "Blonde on Blonde" and the whole bunch is supposed to be very, very good. Their first album is due almost immediately.

Going back to marriage for a moment, we've lost Steve Miller to a beautiful and lucky chick named Kim. They were married a few weeks ago.

The Bopper himself, Mark Lindsay, just about broke his neck the

other night. He's moved into his hillside house which he calls his "hutch" (it's really a four-bedroom brick house on top of a mountain, surrounded by vines and flowers and trees and birds and all). Across one of the doors, Mark has placed one of those gym-type bars (hic) which he does pull-ups on. Well, the bar came crashing down in the middle of one of his exercise snits, and hit him right on the former head! Would you believe he was unconscious for nearly two hours? Lord, everyone was really worried sick. But he's all right now, so don't start sending flowers.

The Raiders are doing very well with their ABC-TV shows, even if same aren't exactly receiving critical acclaim. Freddy Weller has been wowing everyone with his two best-selling CW albums, with (Continued on Page 73)

5

I don't know what publication this came from but it is just as well because they misspelled Ron Kass's last name. Unforgivable! We did have our work cut out for us at MGM, or as we called it, the "Looney Lion's Den."

Paul's visit was relatively unexpected; one might say it was an out and out surprise. Capitol Records was holding its annual convention at the Century Plaza hotel with its executives and promotion men from all over the country, all having a good convention time, when in walked . . . Paul McCartney??! Celebrities and employees alike lined up to have photos taken with the Beatle, who smiled graciously while signing endless autographs for endless pictures, endearing himself forever and ever to all those conventioneers.

Actually, Paul didn't fly several thousand miles just to sign autographs (although it isn't the worst idea anyone ever had). He had to firm up the deal between the Beatles' new Apple Records and Capitol, which will be handling the manufacture and distribution of Apple records in this country and Canada, starting with the Beatles' next album. He wanted to meet the people he would be working with, wanted to get acquainted with the business side of things (and also managed to work in a few leisure hours . . .). The idea of a Businesslike Beatle may be new and strange to us, but we're not about to complain because it will probably mean more Beatle trips to this country, and the more of those the better!

Paul arrived on a Thursday night and stayed until the next Monday afternoon. He stayed at the Beverly Hills hotel and was even listed in the registry there. As he walked in, a kid stopped him in the lobby and asked, "Hey, aren't you John Lennon?" Paul answered, "No, I'm Stevie Wonder."

Although there was no real attempt to hide the fact that he was here, it wasn't generally known, except by a handful of faithful girls who tracked down the rumor and waited patiently outside his bungalow. At first he was smuggled into places, like the convention, for a surprise effect, but after the first day or two he strolled about in plain view of anyone who was watching, pulling up to **front** doors (A welcome change; he commented that all he had seen of this country for the past three years was "back doors and kitchens.")

His wandering took him to

several boutiques, the Whisky A Go Go (where Albert King was playing), the Factory (a private club), and Billy Graham's yacht. But no sooner did he board the boat and leave the pier than the rudder broke and they had to go back for repairs.

Capitol people Ken Mansfield and Larry Delaney spent hours and hours with Paul (being completely charmed by him). "He was always so courteous, no matter how hectic it was," they remember with awe. "He had time for everyone."

Paul with Ken Mansfield

One night the three of them were sitting in Paul's bungalow and Paul took out his guitar and played some tunes which will be on the next album. "He started writing a song and asked **us** for help! But he really listens, he wasn't just being polite." Apparently all the songs have been written for the album, but only a couple have been recorded. "They're not exactly straight yet, but the stuff he played for us was fantastic." Here they groped for the right words. "Artistic . . . pure. More simplicity. How can you describe it?

Not a return to rock and roll, in fact more like the opposite. Beautiful . . ."

The Beatles are in the final stages of constructing their own recording studio at 3 Savile Row in London in the basement of an ancient building. "It's a landmark building, so they have to get permission to make any changes in the structure; that's why the studio has to be in the basement."

Ken and Larry kept remembering anecdotes from Paul's visit, in no particular sequence, events which stuck in their minds. Here are a few:

"Paul couldn't really grasp how the Beatles have affected the American way of life. Every time we'd get into a car after going through a crowd he'd talk about it as if it were a whole new thing to ponder."

"When we took him to the convention we went through the basement and took an elevator to the 15th floor. We were walking down the hall when one of our promo men from Atlanta popped out of a doorway, spotted Paul, stopped dead, then ran up to him and gave him a big hug and said, 'Hey man, howarya, how's it goin?' Paul hugged him right back, saying, 'Hey, great to see ya, how's it goin?' When the guy finally went on down the hall, we asked Paul if he knew him. Paul said he'd never seen him before."

"One morning Paul went down to the hotel pool. There was a guy there who was determined not to be impressed by a Beatle. He walked past Paul and said, very high handedly, 'How are **you?'** Paul replied, 'Fine, how are you?' The guy keep right on walking; Paul leaned forward and called out, 'Hey, you didn't tell me how you were!' Broke everyone up."

"A girl reporter for a TV station was giving him a hard time, but he kept smiling. He was never once as rude as he had a right to be."

"When we took him to the airport to catch his 1:15 flight to London, there was a 3-hour delay because of a bomb threat on his plane. So we stood by the elevator and ate hot dogs and admired pretty girls and blew everyone's mind. I mean, how often do you see Paul McCartney standing at a counter putting mustard on a hot dog??"

Not nearly often enough.

This is a page out of one of the many 1968 teen "fanzines." I like that the article's caption reads Paul *with* Ken Mansfield instead of the other way around. Behind me is Ivan Vaughan, Paul's classmate (Liverpool Institute) from his early years, and traveling mate on Paul's trip to LA. This is a great example of Paul's loyalty to old friends.

Jack Oliver and Tony Bramwell in their ground floor office meeting with staffer Sally Burgess. Jack and Tony were later moved to another office when John and Yoko decided they wanted this space in place of the one they had been occupying. Photo by Tommy Hanley.

Peter Asher at his desk in his fifth floor office—the floor directly below the rooftop concert. The ceiling had been braced shortly before the concert so the whole affair wouldn't come crashing down on him and Chris O'Dell. That's Chris sitting in the corner chair with an unidentified person. Photo by Tommy Hanley.

Claudine Longet & Mal Evans
(left: facing). Pattie Harrison &
Jack Oliver (right: backs turned).

Ricky and Kris Nelson, me in the
middle, Pattie and George Harrison.

George pulled me aside to give advice on
my new venture. He shared his pattern
and tailor for the white suit I'm wearing,
the same one he wore for Bangla Desh.

This was special for me having
my two best friends meet…the
Englishman and the outlaw.
Gentle Mal Evans and wild
Waylon Jennings!

I threw a big party at a remote 7,000-acre ranch
in the Malibu Mountains five years after leaving
Apple to introduce my new company Hometown
Productions Inc. Among the guests attending
were George and Pattie Harrison, Jack Oliver,
Mal Evans, Ricky and Kristin Nelson, Waylon
Jennings, Jessi Colter, Rob Reiner, Penny Mar-
shall, Jennifer Warnes, and Claudine Longet. The
photographer was Leonard Nimoy…yes, that's
Spock with the camera.

I was invited by Crème Tangerine, my favorite Beatles tribute band, to join them for a 40th anniversary rooftop concert celebration in the heart of downtown Seattle. I had always turned these offers down in the past, but I accepted this time because of our friendship.

When I was led out through a door onto a balcony overlooking Pike Place Fish Market area. I was stunned to see the mass of people there. The crowd was so large it overflowed into surrounding streets and backed up traffic for blocks. There was so much happiness and joy in the crowd that I was really glad I went.

Derek Taylor was one of the organizers and Paul McCartney was on the Board of Governors for the Monterey Pop Festival in 1967. The Beatles declined appearing, but all four Beatles did create an original illustration titled "Peace to Monterey" for the $3.00 program. The original sold in 2015 for $175,000.

This was the view from our seats. On stage is Janis Joplin with Big Brother and the Holding Company. Notice how simple the staging was back in those days—it was all about the music. It's interesting to note the same thing about the Beatles' concerts. Unfortunately, in their case, it became all about the noise!

John Lennon and Yoko Ono seated at their shared desk in their ground floor office. I always felt very intimidated when seated before them especially when John wasn't happy. Getty Images Photo.

This picture was taken in the Apple basement studio before it was in full bloom. At first I thought it was a nondescript band rehearsing but upon further observation, Jack Oliver noted that it might be James Taylor facing the camera. Photo by Tommy Hanley.

Apple

```
Ken Mansfield,
Capitol Record Distributing Co.
The Capitol Tower,
Hollywood,
California 90028.
U.S.A.
```

20th March, 1969   carge

Dear Ken,

With reference to the Iveys album front cover, large
cameo with the 4 cut-out heads.

Further to seeing a first proof from the original artwork we are making certain corrections to ensure that
the general background in the cameo should now be, say,
90% of the fifth colour green with the existing black
which will automatically come from the grey background.
Regarding the heads being in two colours green and black
we found that the black and green gave a strong blackish
contrast. We, therefore, decided to reduce the black
on the heads to 30% (approx) with the black at the
(bust-line) (neck-line) totally reduced.   The effect
of this would be that the hard lines which appear at
the base of each head will blend totally with the
background which is now practically solid green.

We will send a proof of this showing these amendments
as soon as possible. We enclose the first proof for
your attention.

Yours sincerely,

JACK OLIVER

Apple Corps Ltd., 3 Savile Row, London, W.1. 01-734 8232. Cables Apcore London, W.1.   Director, N. S. Aspinall.

This is an example of the everyday correspondence that carried on between Jack Oliver and me, showing that we did do actual work at Apple. Of course, The Iveys in time became Badfinger. When I heard their first single I knew they were a hit group with good material and so I instructed Capitol to press the unheard-of amount of 400,000 copies in anticipation of giant sales. I doubt we sold a tenth of that. I was wrong about the single but right about the band. The Beatles liked my enthusiasm for the project, so Capitol quietly ignored my financial blunder, and me and my new UK mates kept on truckin'!

The Beatles, the Bible and Bodega Bay, my first book, on top of a stack in a glass case placed in the entry area of Abercrombie & Fitch at 3 Savile Row that had been set aside as a tribute to the Beatles being a former owner of the building. I have no idea how it got there, but I loved being on top of the pile!

Jack Oliver in front of the new Abercrombie & Fitch where Apple used to be. Jack shared these photos taken in 2015 during his annual trek back home to visit his old stomping grounds. Seeing that street sign always stirs up something deep inside me.

Mal and me on a train ride from Philadelphia to NYC on our way to Jackie Lomax's next event. Our friendship had already deepened but I think the long intense hours on the road handling Jackie's promotional tour brought us even closer together. This was Apple so we enjoyed first class everything including our private digs on the train. Jackie was sitting across from us noodling on his guitar plugged into a tiny battery-operated amp. When he looked up and saw us hard at work, he took this picture. Photo by Jackie Lomax.

© BeatlesPhotos.de

This picture was taken at the famous Sunset Strip Playboy Club…how cool was that (well it was in those days)? George and I are presenting the Golden Apple award to West Coast promo man Don Grierson and clowning around as we are going about it. Mal Evans is seated lower left and Don is seated lower right.

I stumbled across this photo taken while I was on location filming a promotional video for Capitol country artist Buck Owens. This picture was taken not long after I put Paul on the TWA flight to London and before I was asked to join Apple. I noticed in this photo I was still wearing the medallion Paul had given me when we said goodbye at LAX. I wore that prized possession every day until it literally disintegrated from use.

Welcome **TWA** to the world of Trans World Airlines·

POST CARD

USE AIR MAIL

To Kenneth
Dear Kenneth,
Thanks Ken, you're
a pal, Kenny
love from
Paul, Ron, Ive
and Tony

*Service mark owned exclusively by Trans World Airlines, Inc.

Paul wrote this postcard on that TWA flight from L.A. to London (via New York City) after I had taken him to the airport. Upon his return to the UK he put it in an envelope and sent it regular mail from the Apple offices, thus no postmark. This is another example of how accepted he and the band made me feel when they brought me aboard. *(Ron, Ive, and Tony mean Ron Kass, Ivan Vaughan, and Tony Bramwell.)*

I never thought about it until I began gathering pictures for this book. When it comes to "selfies" he was way out in front, taking them over forty years ago. Ringo would often grab us, hold out his camera and snap our picture. He spent almost every day of his life back then dodging photographers but when we were alone he was the one who wanted to take a picture with him in it. Here are three of my favorites.

Top: Me, Alan Pariser, and Ringo during a Party at my place, the legendary "Hangover House," in Laurel Canyon, 1970s.

Middle: Keith Allison, me, and Ringo at one of his annual New Year's Eve parties at his Haslam Terrace home in the Hollywood Hills. 1980s.

Bottom: Me, Bruce Grakal, and Ringo after a long day of shooting publicity pictures for his Private Music (RCA) *Time Takes Time* album. Thirty-five years had passed since we met and we were still working together. This selfie was taken during a private party that evening at the record company's Beverly Hills offices. 1990s.

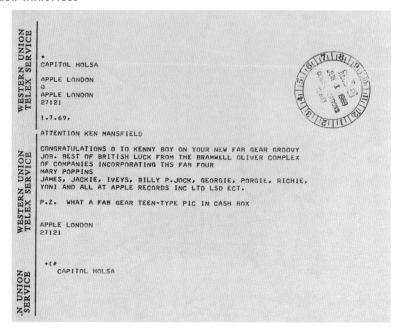

For those who have never seen one of these it is called a telegram. You could receive it the same day it was sent no matter how far away. Amazing! Humor was imbedded in almost everything the crew in London came up with. It softened the chaos and its relevant stress at times.

I received several of these 1969 Apple Christmas cards from the gang at 3 Savile Row. Of course, this one from Mal in 1969 will always be my favorite.

ENDNOTES

i   http://www.telegraph.co.uk/finance/property/invest-
    ment/10836954/How-did-Mayfair-become-Londons-
    most-desirable-area.html

ii https://wetherell.co.uk/mayfair-book/

iii https://www.guitarplayer.com/players/the-beatles-last-
    show-alan-parsons-eyewitness

iiii http://articles.latimes.com/2011/nov/23/entertain-
    ment/la-et-michael-lindsay-hogg-20111123

ACKNOWLEDGMENTS

CONTRIBUTING EDITOR
MARSHALL TERRILL

Before I began writing this book, I asked long-time pal and literary associate Marshall Terrill to ride shotgun as I ventured back in time and relived being a small part of the phenomenon created by the Beatles. As I finished each chapter, I would pass it on to Marshall and, at that point, we would open a constructive dialogue and begin exchanging ideas until each segment was properly polished, creatively embellished, occasionally gutted, and then diligently put in order. It not only took dedication for Marshall to enter and spend hours in the confined space of my mind, but keeping me focused required a lot of patience as well. His contribution to this book is greatly appreciated. Imagine the comfort I enjoyed knowing I had a learned author of over twenty books accompanying me on this journey. It took us a year, but we made it, and we ended up just as we started…good friends. Thanks mate, that's just what I needed…a little help from a friend!

Marshall is a veteran film, sports, and music writer and the author of more than twenty books, including bestselling biographies of Steve McQueen, Elvis Presley, and Pete Maravich. In 2017, he served as executive producer of *Steve McQueen: American Rebel*, a faith-based film documentary. He resides in Tempe, Arizona. www.marshallterrill.com

HISTORICAL CONSULTANTS

I remember the essence of moments very clearly because the things that remain in my selective memory are those that impressed my inner being. I do have a prevailing problem with sequence, location, historical facts, and even faces; but, with a great group of friends who have the gift of valid content, I have been kept on the recollection rails in my portrayals and ramblings. In addition to Marshall's oversight and contributions, I invited these talented authors who know all things Beatles to check my facts to make sure they are in order. Before this book reached the printer, these four men examined the manuscript for authenticity and even gave me some of their words. In writing about the Beatles, there are a lot of hard-held opinions about various events, so in those instances of data variance, instead of debating minutiae—a battle I will surely lose—I have proceeded only when they agreed my stance was sure. If any fact was debatable, I have either left it out or gone vague on detail, leaning instead on just recalling the special feeling of being there. It is their books that are to be read if you seek a deeper, objective understanding of the lads from Liverpool. Thanks guys for putting the cap back on the truth paste when I tried squeezing too much out of some situations.

Bruce Spizer

World-renowned Beatles historian/expert and Beatles projects consultant for Universal Music Group, Capitol Records, and Apple Corps, Ltd. He's author of nine critically acclaimed books including *The Beatles are Coming! The Birth of Beatlemania in America* and *The Beatles and Sgt. Pepper: A Fans' Perspective*—all available through his website www. beatle.net, internet sellers, and book stores.

Mark Lewisohn

The acknowledged world authority on the Beatles, Mark's many books include the bestselling and *influential Recording Sessions, The Complete Beatles Chronicle*, and was a consultant and researcher for all aspects—TV, DVDs, CDs and book—of the Beatles' own Anthology. For more information on his extensive body of works visit http://www.marklewisohn.net. Thoroughly British, Mark lives to write in the UK.

Robert Rodriguez
Respected Beatles scholar; award-winning author (Revolver: How the Beatles Re-Imagined Rock 'n' Roll); public speaker and creator-host of the acclaimed "Something About the Beatles" podcast. www.somethingabout-thebeatles.com He lives outside Chicago with his wife and kids.

Stefan Granados
Author of *Those Were the Days: The History of Apple Records*. He is also a Producer for the UK reissue label RPM Records/Cherry Red Records, for whom he has curated the Apple Music Publishing compilation CD series, as well as worked with Apple Corps on the reissues of albums by Lon and Derek Van Eaton, Grapefruit, and Mortimer.

General Editor
Cara Highsmith
This is my seventh published book, and the second time Cara Highsmith has joined me in the final editing of my impassioned affair with words, semantics, and even some antics. Literary rubber met the road, a sharpened pencil was put to paper, and Ken the author met Cara the authority of this scholarly craft when I handed her what I deemed a finished manuscript. She took my story in hand *and* in heart and became immersed in the project. When she was finished, *The Roof*'s debris was cleared and the Apple was polished. Correct myself if I is wrong but there ain't not none better editor anywheres.

Cara Highsmith holds a Master of Arts in English and has worked in publishing in several areas, including the editorial team at Hachette Book Group USA working with several *New York Times* bestselling authors. After leaving Hachette in 2008, she launched her own company (www.highsmithcreativeservices.com) providing writing, editing, and self-publishing consultation services. She lives in Los Angeles, CA.

SPECIAL ACKNOWLEDGEMENT

Brent Stoker

This is my third book about the Beatles. Brent served as Contributing Editor on my first two: *The Beatles, the Bible, and Bodega Bay* and *The White Book*. He labored at great lengths on both of those offerings and segments of information for *The Roof: The Beatles' Final Concert* are derivatives of those original efforts. This time I wanted him to enjoy the ride without schedules and obligations, so I asked him to write one chapter that I felt he was uniquely qualified to do. *And the Band Played On* was his baby all the way. My contribution was less than minimal and admittedly perfunctory. Thanks, Brent. It wouldn't have been the same without you. Just like old times…eh?

MOST APPRECIATIVE
ACKNOWLEDGEMENT POSSIBLE

Brian Mitchell has come alongside me on my author's journey, becoming not only a great friend; but, because he cares he has moved to the front of my life in leading the way so that my stories could find their way into your hands. He and Bill Reeves of Working Title Agency have given my words a safe home to live and also found a great place for them to land…Post Hill Press with Michael Wilson, a publisher who cares.

Speaking of safe places and caring…God bless you, Connie. I love that you chose "Mama He's Crazy" as our song when we were dating. That was over thirty years ago and here we are…still safe, caring, and crazy in love. I might also mention there's another song—the one that we chose together for our wedding: "You're a Gift from God to Me."

ALSO BY KEN MANSFIELD

The Beatles, The Bible, and Bodega Bay

The White Book

Between Wyomings

Stumbling on Open Ground

Rock and a Heart Place

Philco